Letters to God from a Former Atheist

Jason D. Hill, Ph.D.

Letters to God from a Former Atheist

HIS✝RIA
CHRISTIAN

Histria Christian

Las Vegas ♦ Chicago ♦ Palm Beach

Published in the United States of America by
Histria Books
7181 N. Hualapai Way, Ste. 130-86
Las Vegas, NV 89166 U.S.A.
HistriaBooks.com

Histria Christian is an imprint of Histria Books dedicated to books that embody and promote Christian values and an understanding of the Christian faith. Titles published under the imprints of Histria Books are distributed worldwide.

Library of Congress Control Number: 2024944042

ISBN 978-1-59211-510-5 (hardcover)
ISBN 978-1-59211-525-9 (eBook)

In memory of my late grandmother, Ivy Polack,
Who taught me how to pray

Introduction

At some point in my late teens, I became an atheist.

I do not remember the exact moment when it happened. I was raised as a Roman Catholic in a fairly religious middle-class Jamaican household. My atheism was born a year and a half before I migrated to the United States at the age of twenty in 1985. And strange as this might sound, my disbelief seemed like a gift from God. What better way to enter a wonderful country where I would inherit a new world and make a new life for myself, than with a clear and distinct mind devoid of superstitious beliefs about an ineffable God who resided in some translucent sky. The decision to become a writer and a philosopher gave my atheism the principled vocational dignity I thought it deserved.

I relished in the new freedom I found in my intransigent atheism. A surge of autonomy and a sense of power seized me in a way that I thought was possible only in dreams of flying. I felt what, in retrospect, was a false sense of invulnerability where things happened simply because I willed them. I never lost my moral compass; however, I did hubristically take on the demeanor of being like a God unto myself. The feeling of empowerment was intoxicating.

At some point in my early to mid-thirties, my atheism began to undo itself—despite my best efforts to the contrary! The intensity and conceptual haziness of that experience is now ripe for the telling, which I shall do in great detail at the end of this book. Truth be told, it betrays all thought I have right now, despite the fact that, as an academic philosopher, I prize thinking as my most celebrated way of functioning in the world. Today, I see that living in Faith with the Lord is not incompatible with reason. If man is endowed with reason, and if he is made in the image of God, then reason is a supreme attribute of God. It is from Him that we inherit this rational faculty.

Despite my reluctance and my panic at the loss of my self-image as a free-thinking atheist, my disbelief dissipated, and I found myself in the occasional throes of deep religious sensibilities for which I had no explanation. I would, for example, find myself giving in to a passionate urge to literally crawl into a church at 2 a.m. and simply sit there, allowing myself to be flooded with sensations that can only be described as religious, or spiritual, except they were more than that.

Silently, relentlessly, the notion that atheism was no longer an option I could live with pressed itself into my thoughts. But the newfound release from atheism was short-lived. For the next decade a battle waged deep inside my soul; I traversed the irreconcilable states of belief and disbelief. One moment God felt so close I could almost feel Him next to me. The next moment the universe felt devoid of His presence and, often, despite having found love, and worldly success, I was possessed of a sinking void and emptiness that today I know with full certainty that only the Lord can fill. But I willed myself to believe. I needed to believe. Need was not enough. I adopted elaborate rituals and practices which played an invaluable role in strengthening my spiritual core. But faith eluded me. I cried out to Jesus while denying He was the Son of God in my heart. The universe's answer seemed to be: Silence!

I have battled deeply with this project, not knowing what to do with it, feeling like a fake for writing it, knowing that my spiritual life and any chance for happiness were doomed without pursuing it. In another book, I had stated that I wrote to become the person I would like to be. In the midst of much professional success, when all my dreams were coming true and when I had love in many forms, I found myself desperately unhappy. Emptiness and an insatiable hollowness accompanied by intense anxiety attacks overcame me. Migraine headaches seized me with an unrelenting ferocity I found increasingly harder to withstand. I had been trying to recover a prayer life for years but felt deeply unsuccessful in my endeavors. At each attempt, reason would take over, and the conceptual man would chastise the boy in quest of Biblical awakening. I thought myself foolish for attempting to pray to an ineffable being.

Driving in my truck one morning on my way to teach logic classes at a small midwestern university, over two decades ago, my entire thought process suddenly came to a halt. I was confronted with a set of questions that seemed to emerge from nowhere. A voice said to me: "What is the talent that I have given you, the one thing without which you mistakenly believe your life would be not worth living?" The answer that came immediately?

Writing.

"If you are having difficulties praying to me," the voice continued, implacably and calmly, "then why not use the talent I gave you to pray? Use your writing as a form of prayer. Write me letters."

Such is the genesis of this project. I nearly crashed my truck as I sped up to reach my office to begin the letters, two of which had already written themselves in my mind.

So much for the preparation of logic for my morning class. I winged it, so to speak, in delirious ecstasy. I have been writing these letters to God for more than twenty-two years now. I have deleted many because I have felt that I was not worthy of even uttering His name, let alone asking for grace. I have added to the ones I deleted asking God and Jesus and the Holy Spirit to write new prayers in my heart.

I have always felt that my vocation as a writer—whether expressed in academic philosophy, fiction, or essays—ought to be pursued for the sake of truth as opposed to self-centered indulgence. If I feel like a fool in the process, if my body is racked with doubts as I write, then, in the name of my highest goal—truth—I must carry on.

I seek no status and claim no special visionary insight. My soul has felt incomplete from as far back as I can remember myself. I have been searching for its completion all my life. I cried out to God, and deep in my heart, I would like to believe that after years of desperation, perhaps, He granted me a small dose of grace. I am just beginning to develop faith and am thus still an infant in this respect. This book is meant for those who love prayer, for those who want to look into the soul of a man who projected bravado and supreme confidence to the world, but whose soul has been shattered at various points; for those who want to witness the manner in which, through prayer and surrender, that soul is in a deep healing process; for those who doubt and are losing faith and would like to believe there is hope— There is! And simply: for any person who just loves the Lord and exalts in seeing His name glorified for none other than for His own sake. This book is yours.

I write as a work in progress, or, as a recovering atheist. I use the term recovering because I think the journey back to God will take a lifetime to accomplish. I simply offer these letters in a spirit of sharing, to let the reader witness the spectacle of spiritual desperation and the driving need to find the anchor in my life I cavalierly tossed aside.

In Easter of 2019, I went to a Good Friday service and contemplated the Cross for a long time. I went up to it as did most of the congregants, and I prayed to God that He would allow me to grant Jesus entrance into my life. I told him I was not there yet. But I was desperate. I was humbled, and I needed to be a supplicant in His Holy service. I closed my eyes and bowed my head in prayer in my seat and cried—wondering if God had heard me.

Two days later, on Easter Sunday, I returned to the same church with excitement. I don't know why I felt excited, but a surge of vitality coursed its way through my body. During the beautiful service the pastor asked the congregants to meditate on what he was about to tell us. I did. And it changed my life. He said right now, in this moment, the tomb of the original Buddha was occupied because his bones were still there. He said the tomb of Mohammed was occupied because his bones were still there. Then he paused for a while and smiled kindly and said: "The tomb of Christ is empty for he has risen." Unconsciously, channeled by the Holy Spirit I fell to my knees, cried, and gave my life to Jesus and accepted Him as my Lord and Savior. The ensuing prayers will reveal the magic of that moment, so, I won't spoil it for you.

God is alive!

What will the process be like and how will it all end? I know not, and I care not. My life has been given to me and I know that I must satisfy the cries of a soul I am just beginning to glimpse, a soul whose face often eludes me.

To write in this way is to render a disservice to the feelings towards a God whom I have respected, despised, and then seriously ceased to believe in. It is a disservice because while I believe that the capacity for feelings and emotions are infinite, our linguistic vocabulary is not. Conceptually speaking, I am handicapped since the concepts and words used to express thoughts cannot, in this case, capture the nuances, the depth and the awesome feelings that rack a soul that searched for

God. But I continue because I am driven to write out of sheer necessity: I could no more stop writing than I could stop breathing. The words are intimations, and they offer a small glimpse into a desperate and tenacious soul at work.

I worked on the letters intermittently by transcribing them from my prayer journal. The final experience that committed me to keep at it, so to speak, to never abandon God, happened during a near-death experience I had. During a minor surgical procedure that went awry, I aspirated in the recovery room and almost drowned in my own blood. I heard one doctor say: "We are going to lose him." Another asked: "Is he gone?"

I felt as if I were being held under water and desperately wanted to come up for air. I heard another doctor pleading with me: "Breathe Mr. Hill. Please, breathe."

But I could not breathe. How ironic it all was. In the fifteen months preceding my surgery I had experienced the most agonizing anxiety attacks and had fantasized about death as a source of comfort. I had romanticized the suicide of the confessional poets Anne Sexton and Sylvia Plath whose works I admired. I had even envied them for their courage in taking their lives.

Truth be told, I was planning on committing suicide. In these letters, prayers, and devotionals you will see how He came to my rescue.

As I felt my life slipping away in the recovery room and knew that my weakening body was failing to summon up the strength to do the one thing that comes naturally for most of us—inhaling a small breath of air—I knew that I did not want to die. I did not think of the numerous books I wanted to write or of how many people would miss me if I died. I had no sentimental thoughts in my mind at all. I knew instantaneously that life, this thing, my life, no matter how hard, difficult, and tortured it was, was worth living. I knew that I'd rather spend the rest of my days holding on to a tortured existence and live trying to figure out what to really do with it, than to relinquish it because it would be the end of strife and suffering. In that moment, I did not panic. I saw very clearly that this phenomenon called life—that I, perhaps so many of us, fool around with—could snap like a dried-up twig. I wanted it back. Now I am convinced that the spirit of Jesus entered my body and gave me strength. I breathed and splattered everything and everyone around me with blood. I spent the next two months re-building my body back to life. It was then that I began mouthing every day to God my daily mantra: *Thank You God for my life here on earth. And thank You for my existence.*

My life was given back to me, and, in return, I cherished every day despite repeated setbacks and further hospitalizations during that year for serious blood clots in both lungs as well as a serious case of viral meningitis.

I was alive and that was all that mattered.

But the joy was not to last. In the ensuing years I lapsed into a deep suicidal depression. In that space I steadfastly pursued a morbid and romantic fascination with death. I would not say that my atheism returned; rather, I considered God way beyond my reach and I beyond His range of vision. In the end, I rejected the curious call of death and checked myself into the psychiatric ward of a hospital close to my home.

I did not ask for any signs this time. To live is a decision. I made a decision to stop inhaling death. I returned to the letters. And in the return, more signs of God's presence revealed themselves to me.

I no longer pray for "things" in our fallen world. I pray each morning, instead, for God to teach me what my prayer for the day should be. I ask that I forever lean into His understanding. And I ask Him to give me the grace and the courage to accept His will and plan for my life as the highest good that could ever possibly exist for me here on earth.

"You called and cried out loud and shattered my deafness. You were radiant and resplendent, you put to flight my blindness. You were fragrant, and I drew in my breath and now pant after. I tasted you, and I feel but hunger and thirst for you. You touched me, and I am set on fire to attain the peace which is yours."[1]

---

[1] Augustine—The Confession X.xxvii (38)—Translated with an introduction by Henry Chadwick

Dear God:

I am about to embark on this incredible journey, and I am afraid. I am afraid because for most of my life as a child I have known You. I worshipped You. I adored You. At some point I turned away from You. I repudiated You. Like the father who cast me aside when I was a child and broke my heart by sacrificing his sons to serve You, I also abandoned You. I was angry because You stole the man I loved, the man who played with me and held me close to his side. He was my father, and You stole him. Well, this was my accusation against You for almost two decades.

He left us all when we were so young, and I was so desperate for the love of a father. He left me when the hunger in my soul for emotional and psychological visibility threatened to devour me. He left me when the soul You gave me yearned to express itself as an artist, a writer, and all around me said: "That is not the way." Everyone but my father, my dad. God, do You remember the times he would take me for long drives, when he would clutch me and weep, for he too was a lost lamb, a desperate soul who wanted to invigorate the world with his mad inebriated vision and the world told him he was a fool? He had lost his battles, tried to take his own life and here he was, telling me that I was to be a writer, that I would find my uniform in Christ's vision, and that I was special. And we wept together, often. And I loved him. Do You remember the day I wrapped my legs around his waist and kissed him all over his neck and he told his mother: I think my son is in love with me? And then, God, one day, he left us. The world said he had schizophrenia, he said he had seen Your face and had been called out to be Your servant and, with these words, he left us:

My Sons, Oh my Sons.

How do I regret time was too short to

Kiss your sweat while we played.

Born prematurely old

I was called out to war;

Vanity was not my cause

Nor the cause of my Requiem.

So although the past remains a haunting cancerous memory

It is unwise to resurrect,

A cold deliberate casualty

Fired with the blood wrung from our twisted souls.

I trod the king's highway towards the souls I left behind.

Solitude is my way out of madness, my children.

Loneliness is a triumphant man.

Meanwhile, my God, I cried out to You for six years every night to come and take his place. I walked from school alone, and prayed on behalf of others because I was too afraid to pray for myself after disappointment and shame had overwhelmed me. I asked You to deliver one crumb of happiness inside the heart of each child in the world. I prayed: "Let each child experience just one minute of complete fullness and happiness and remember it when he or she is sad."

Dear God:

Release me from the need of respectability. Release me from the prying eyes of others. Help me to dispel the obsession with wearing the masks I don each morning as I face the world. Let me grow in Your image and let that, oh God, be the only mask I wear. Let that image implant itself in the deepest labyrinths of my soul, let it permeate my thoughts, my subconscious. Let it be part of the way I love my family, my friends, the world, and myself. Grant me the courage to stand before the world and say: This is who I am. Give me the courage to bear the consequences and the conviction of knowing that as Your child, who I am is what I am supposed to be.

Thank you for all that I ask for. If I should not receive that for which I ask, thank you for the kindness in not granting those things that were never mine to be had in the first place.

God:

Sometimes I wake up in the morning and wish that I did not have to rise out of bed. Sometimes the weight of the world crushes me, and I feel in my heart that You are never there. Take this passivity from my soul, God, and grant me the maturity to seek You out the way I seek all the earthly things I desire in my life. I sometimes wonder, God, why is it that someone as aggressive, as willful as myself, who has, with dogged determination, pursued everything he wanted, why when it comes to You, I sit passively? Waiting. Waiting. Waiting. Waiting for You to come to me. Am I ungrateful then for not using the strengths You have given me? I have two legs to carry my body, a mind to outsmart those I fear, and yet, I use not my mind nor my heart to seek you out, to pursue You the way I would pursue someone I truly loved, or a person I wanted as a friend. Forgive me God. It is fear that sometimes rules my heart. I fear that You will not listen to me, that You will not hear me and that You will not grant the things I ask for. Flood me with the courage to make that leap of faith into the unknown.

Help me to know the difference between abandonment and contemplative silence. I want to contemplate my life with You each morning and, to find in that contemplation, serenity of mind and conviction of principle.

God, I am rising from my bed and taking those steps into the world You have placed me in to be fruitful and productive.

God, thank You for the spirit of discernment that recognizes your presence in the midst of loneliness and abandonment. I feel pain in my heart, anger in my veins. But I am not numb. My body pulsates with life, my heart is never still and so I feel: You are there.

I am still sluggish; my body is operating below the level at which it was prescribed to function at birth. I am cursing the wind as I make another entrance into a world I feel alienated from.

Thank You, God, for the capacity to walk into that world. I am alive today, and You and I have the power to create the world anew.

God:

Sometimes we ask You for things and we do not get them, and then we turn away from You in despair and anger. I wonder, God, if the problem has to do with our state of mind when we come to You.

We would not offer a guest a glass of water polluted with dirt, or feed her rice sprinkled with poison, or prepare a feast for our children in unwashed pots. But observe our manner of approach to You for the things we desire: hearts filled with anger; and souls tormented by greed and acquisitive thoughts. We sully the sanctity of prayer by burdening it with the egomaniacal desires of power to rule the souls of others and to win them over. We empty the debris and detritus of our souls on to You like we empty garbage into open space, or filth in a sewer. I have an image, God, of an innocent child carrying a glass of water to her father. She is three and she has prepared the water herself, taking pains to make sure that the glass is clean and the water pure. She hands it to him with love. There is a smile; the sweetest of smiles spreading around her mouth like the first etches of spring as it spreads its warming touches around a solitary tree. And the smile spreads, Oh Lord, as she watches him quench this thirst.

I would like to be that child, Lord, and when I pray, I want to come to You with the cleanliness of heart that is just and seeks one wish: to do your will.

Dear God:

Come into my heart today. Whisper in my ear the way a lover would. Embrace me with Your presence as if You are in love with me. Soothe my fears as would my mother. Stroke my ego and let it dissipate into Your hands. Command me to rise in the name of Your Holy Will so that You and I become an invincible team. Reconcile my will with Yours so I see the foolishness of heart that is at the center of my battles in the world.

Wed Your spirit to mine, dear God, so that my desperate struggle for my soul culminates in reunion with you. You are my soulmate, and You will fill me up, bring the fullness and completeness to my life I so desperately seek from others. God, You have peered into my soul and seen the darkness that hangs like night, the sadness perched there arrogantly like an unwanted squatter, the terror that seizes me. You also see the passion for life and the drive to conquer. And You have looked into my soul and seen the righteousness and pride I bore in relation to my suffering, hanging on to it like a mother who clings to the dead body of her only child. <u>She cannot move on because her tragedy is her only authentic possession.</u> All these things You have seen, Lord. I know that I shall rise. I simply have to rise.

God:

Loneliness has plagued me most of my life. Today, however, I thought for the first time that I deserved loneliness. Perhaps we all do. I think of the Indian philosopher Judi Krishnamurti. Remember what he said? *That our souls do not have relationships. Our images do.*

In relation to our fellow human beings, this is how we speak:

I have an image of you. You have an image of me. I have an image of myself that I thrust on to the world, an image I must guard and manage. We sit at the table and what do we bring to the table? I introduce my image to you, you present yours. You say something and my image responds. You move me in some way, and I fear to show you how I feel. I fear I will appear weak and sensitive. So I feign a response. The response emanates from my image and from my persona.

We play this game all our lives, never stopping for a moment to witness the violence we do to the soul by starving it, by refusing it expression. We confuse the image for who we are and at the end of the day we retract the images and bury them deep in the labyrinths of our souls. Our images meet. Our souls remain hidden.

We deserve our loneliness, God. We deserve it. We are cowards. I am a coward. I have not grown up. Until I do, and until I have the humanity to bare my soul and expose its needs, its hunger, and its vulnerability, I have no right for visibility and authentic human contact. Until I learn that the image is not who I am, then I have no right not to feel dejected. I have earned my loneliness, God, for I have made it into me. We all have. Do not pity us, oh God. Do not take away our loneliness. Let us find the courage to expose the soul you gave us. That indestructible soul that can be harmed by no one but the man himself.

God:

Where is the heroic in the human spirit today? Where is the desire to grow out of our solipsistic self-centered universe into something phenomenal? Give us the courage to live, Lord—to live fully. In so doing we will have the courage to die; to face death serenely and with dignity. Give us the courage to die natural deaths to our old selves as we grudgingly live our partial lives. Give us death to the prejudices and the neuroses of others that we internalize as our own.

Give me the strength to disaffirm and disown the person others take me to be and, by default, respect. Give me the courage to strip away the layers of their projections, their hopes and aspirations, their fantasies, and their dreams that they burden me with. Grant me the humility to turn down the heroism others want to foist on me so that they may forgive their own cowardice and, through me, vicariously experience the excellence they have ceased to expect of themselves. Rid me of those moments when I fail to realize that I am complicit in this vicious sado-masochistic chicanery. Let me be aware of the nature of my own impulses. Let me remember that I am not always driven by the pursuit of excellence and honor for their own sake, but rather, to conquer and dominate others with the power of my mind and dwarf them with my achievements. Help me to see when I cry out in loneliness, the ambiguous and unclean motives that drive me to pursue actions that have the best of consequences. Help me to understand why I am left spent, empty and unfulfilled in spite of the consequences. Give me the courage to face the dark side of my own benevolent nature which condemns me to a lifetime of alienation from others even as I effusively give and give of myself in gestures that seem so pure, but that You and I know are meant to seduce others into being my possessions: <u>objects that will love me and never leave me.</u> In those moments grant me the decency of spirit to say: "Lord, I deserve my loneliness, afflictions, and alienation. Give me Your hand and show me a better way. I do what I do because I fear the world, and I fear rejection and abandonment."

God:

Today I felt like a spiritual cannibal. Desperation crept up all over me, all over my body and permeated my thoughts. Incompleteness and a deep abyss in my spirit have plunged me into spiritual avarice. I did not see people today. I did not see flesh and blood brothers and sisters. I saw souls on which I could feed, souls that would provide the fuel I needed to go on.

Where were You today? Today, God, You have gone out of me, bailed out, swift and clean. I do not feel bloodless, but without water, as thirsty as the shells would feel if the Atlantic dried up and left them to bake in the torpid sun.

Or perhaps the question is: <u>Where was I in my search for You today?</u> What prompted me to abandon the search and find it in the worst form of spiritual gluttony? To hack a person's limb off is one thing. To hack a piece of his or her soul is to take something away that no medical prosthesis can rebuild.

I wanted to take away from some today that which only You can give: spiritual life. Why? Was it because I have seen myself as one who has fed others with optimism, and with my certainty that the heroic is possible, and that today I was offered no reciprocation?

Am I <u>that</u> diabolically selfish in my giving, God? Do I give out of soul deprivation, or do I give because my heart is full, and I can't help it any more than I can help breathing? Perhaps a bit of both? Maybe I give for none of these reasons. But I hope that You'll help me to understand this thing of giving.

I am confused.

Sometimes we give to enslave others, to hold them captive to our own needs. I have been like a beast of prey, eyeing the weaknesses of others, a predator filled with love for his victims. I am moved by the plight of their pain, my dripping arteries hungry for what they have to offer but moved enough to create boundaries for them. How often I have warned people about myself, told them how difficult I am, how possessive and jealous I can be. How often I have watched how the hunger in their souls causes them to disregard the warnings and reach out for me.

How often has my own hunger made me the victim of those I thought were mine? How much longer can this game be played?

The false beliefs we hold about ourselves—thinking that we are stronger than we really are; unaware that the hunger and the weakness that drive us to ensnare others will trick us in the end. Like the victim of asphyxiation who has no awareness of his need for air, I sometimes feel that I am unaware of how self-suffocation, forged in the crucibles of the tyranny of my ambition, robs me of my humanity.

Fill me with humanity, dear God, and at least in those moments when I lack it, grant me the insight to recognize the forms of the loathsome things that grow in its place and the moral wisdom to relinquish them.

God:

The issues that plague many of us are: How to remove ourselves from the presence of those whose being in the world offends us? Do we try to change them? And further: those whose freedom we are tempted to violate because we want something from them which, by their constitutional make-up and by the nature of our relationship to them, they cannot fulfill. How do we engage them? How do we wish others well when we are tempted to do otherwise?

I hope we will always have the wisdom to never trespass against the freedom of others. Should friends offend us with words or actions, grant us the insight to point out their transgressions. If other folks' ways of being in the world disturb our inner peace, allow us to use our freedom graciously by quietly removing ourselves from their lives. No fighting words. No hatred. No animosity. And let them see our removal from their lives as a sign of deep respect. Now they can exist without the hindrance of our judgments.

Thank You God:

Thank You for the life of my beloved grandmother as she lies dying. Thank You for the heartbreak she causes me as I continue loving her more and more in her decline. Thank You for the compassion she teaches me as she struggles to reveal her love without being able to speak. Thank You for the humility I sometimes feel as she continues to affirm life while she lies incontinent, paralyzed, and alone in her thoughts. Thank You for the gift of her smile as she struggles to smile on a face ravaged by the violence of a stroke.

Thank You for her gentleness, and that I was able to make her proud of me. Thank You for the wonderful lessons she taught me, for her unrelenting prayers, and for that indomitable spirit under which I took refuge as a child when the bullies came chasing me and I was too afraid to fight back.

God:

Do You create women like her anymore?

I wonder.

I hope so.

My friends and I talk about this all the time. We say: "They don't make women like our grandmothers anymore. They are a dying breed."

How is it, Lord, that in her suffering, this woman, once so vibrant and filled with life, still manages to affirm You and Your life in her refusal to succumb to despair? How is such a phenomenon as *her* possible? I call her a miracle. And I, in my privileged life—made partially possible through my struggle and dedication, but also through her struggle, and my mother's struggle—complain about the loneliness of modern life. I moan over the unfairness of our unjust society. What are my tribulations compared to hers? Yet, she never complains. Steadfastly she holds to the dignity and the wonder with which she started her life. With equanimity she affirms the knowledge that what remains of her life is the best of what she has left here on earth.

Thank You, God, for this greatest of all miracles, my beloved grandmother, my unexpected benevolent gift from the world. I never expected that her powerful silence and the joy from her incandescent eyes would have led me slowly back, back to You.

Dear God:

The Pope, John Paul, was here in St. Louis today. I turned on the television without intending to watch him speak at the Kiel Center, but there he was. And the first words I heard him say were: "You come to know Christ through prayer."

He spoke of the need for a prayer life and of the ways in which discovery of Christ was predicated on this prayer life. It was as if he were speaking directly to me, for here I am trying to know You through a life of prayer.

I was moved by his speech about love and compassion and by the sight of the afflicted children from the children's hospital as they spontaneously genuflected and embraced him around his waist.

And he kissed the top of their heads. They hung on to every word he said as if they relied on the oxygen of his vision for the liberation of their own burgeoning little souls. I was moved, Lord, so moved that I wept Your name many times, and a deep longing came over me.

Thank you, God, for giving me the gift of tears. They spill from my eyes not because I despair. I cry out of great longing and hunger. On my knees, watching the children, my cry was one of jubilation for the plenitude of Your presence. For years I've wanted that presence, and You gave it to me. I repeated the words to You, God. Do You remember those words?

"My God, My God, it's been such a long journey coming home to You, but I am home at last. I've come home to You at last."

And I felt Your arms around me. I felt Your love, the weight of Your expectations and Your destiny for me. I felt scared not because you would abandon me, but because I was afraid that I would not be enough of the man You dreamed that I could be.

Okay, God:

Can you believe it? I stood at a podium today and talked to senior citizens about Christian theology. I felt proud, humbly so, when that wonderful lady told me that, after being a Christian for over thirty years, she felt that I had explained the concept of faith in a deeper and more insightful way than she had ever experienced.

All I had done was perform my role of the secular philosopher.

Thank you, God, for filling my soul with the equanimity of Your Divine Love and Wisdom. Thank You for the rapture of heart I felt in talking about You and the test You put Abraham through. I tried to explain that to them. But now I ask You, why did you do it? Why did You ask Abraham to sacrifice the beloved son he had waited for, for such a long time? You didn't need to feel his love that way. Did You? And You are not the kind of God who needs that kind of obedience from his children in order to feel good about himself, are You? So why?

I want to think about this issue and to see how You attempt to magnify the human spirit and stretch it beyond our boldest imagination.

I've pondered this question the way a philosopher ought to. Then I abandoned the idea of pondering. I examined one of my images of You. I see You in some way as a moral trainer. The athletic trainer pushes his charges almost to the point of breaking, making them feel like they have been placed in the hands of a masochist who has found his calling in the pleasures of inflicting pain in a torture chamber.

The athletic trainer sees the potential of his athlete. He knows what his protégé is capable of in ways that elude the athlete since the latter is so often preoccupied with the immediacy of his own whims, desires, wishes, and dreams.

The trainer, however, sometimes sees the winning picture in its entirety; sometimes he intuits it. Like an intransigent creator, he sets as his life's goal the task of extracting every ounce of endurance and stamina that the athlete possesses to recreate him or her into embodied excellence. The trainer offers up his vision of his athlete as a gift, the gift of his imagination in seeing in his athlete traits that he or she could not have seen. In the end, the torture rack looks like a noble monastery and the trainer an insightful and pretty smart guy. The athlete is thankful that his trainer had the psychological acuity to see beyond the rough and gritty surface of resistance, and simultaneously, had the willpower to remain steadfast in his vocation as a mineralogist of the physical body and human spirit.

You, my God, are the moral trainer in our lives. You test us in ways that we cannot fathom. I have an image of a father in a swimming pool trying to coax his daughter into jumping.

"Just jump in and you'll learn to swim that way." She refuses.

I'll catch you, his eyes communicate. And the child wants to read in those eyes the assurance that she will be caught and saved from drowning. Every precarious fiber of her emerging self-confidence demands it. And she jumps. If she fails to jump, then she will no longer believe she has a father she can trust. If she has no father she can trust, then she is an orphan trapped in a house with the phantom figure of a man who acts like a father. She jumps because she needs to believe that the man in the pool is Father.

My God, my Father, sometimes need is belief, isn't it?

But her father doesn't catch her. She is left to fumble and splash and move her limbs in frantic desperate motions.

She panics, but he coaxes her on.

"You can do it. Don't give up. Don't Panic. I won't let you drown but try to remember everything I taught you about treading water. Remember, and I promise, I won't let you drown."

And her primordial sense of survival needs to not only read trust in those eyes, but a deeper desire to please the father she loves, to honor the simple goodness that resides in him. She needs to honor the father she knows is always on her side. Her head barely above water, she splutters and breathes and, like a grand phoenix rising from the vortex, she summons the heroic within her little spirit and begins to tread. She treads. She is rinsing; rising above the depths that threaten her life, rising by the power of hope and the unmistakable love of her father.

Are You that man for me, God? Are You? I feel You are because need is fast becoming belief. The anguish in my soul drowns the joy I should feel in my professional and material achievements. As I am advancing in the "world" I thought I willed, so I am dissolving inside.

Death.

Not by one apocalyptic blow, rather, a bittersweet death, one where pain and happiness commingle freely, and where I glimpse my own freedom in some distant place. This death is death by thousands of tiny scratches, each bleeding competitively with the other—crazily, every day, every night as I reluctantly lay my head on my pillow.

That is why You ordered Abraham to do what he did. You wanted to give him a majestic gift. You wanted to stretch him morally so that in the end he would emerge a radically different man. You would hand him the most exalted portrait of himself (did he recognize himself after you put him through the test?) and say: "This is how you were intended to be. Here is the highest possible, and here is what you have become. I am proud of you, my son. I am, indeed, very proud of you."

I want to be radically honest with You, God. Really honest. I want You to give me that gift. A part of me wants You to be that moral trainer in my life. But I am afraid. I am so afraid of the challenges You might put me through. I am afraid that I am not strong enough to meet them, or that my faith in You will not withstand the moments I question the sanity of those challenges.

Grant me the faith to accept those challenges You will foist on me, on all of us, really. They are the inescapable conditions of human life. Nothing more. Fill my heart and the hearts of those who want such challenges with the presence of Your spirit. And when we cry out in agony and despair, when we doubt Your existence and Your love, strengthen our vision so that we may see in the benevolent eyes of strangers the compassion we need to go on in the name of Your Plan for our lives. The end for which we were all created.

God:

What does faith mean to me?

I say right now as I struggle to rebuild my relationship with You, that faith is a non-contradictory belief in the supra-rationality of Your decisions and actions in the context of human life (my life) even when those decisions betray comprehensible ways of interpreting the world in which I live. That's me the intellectual talking. And that's me thinking that I can or should protect myself from You as I seek to find You in these letters.

Now, how do I truly see faith? Or how do I experience it?

I experience it humbly, by acknowledging how incomplete and, often, how painful the story of my will has been in the unfolding of my life. It's true that I have micro-managed my life, and that my tenacity and willpower have allowed me to subvert obstacles. But in all honesty, I have come upon so many unexpected paths that have filled my life with unexpected abundance that I must admit that sometimes I feel as if I'm a player on a checkerboard and that You are overseeing the strategies and making the ultimate moves. You make me make my moves according to what seems like my will and then a move that I didn't plan occurs. My life changes. Doors open. Opportunities reveal themselves. I find myself taking journeys my will did not forge. I find myself being rescued from difficult situations in ways that seem miraculous. Deep in my bones, I feel You are there, that You have always been there, that no matter what I do, You will be there making those moves in my life.

God makes moves on me.

I like that.

It makes me feel close to You, like we are partners in a marriage. It is a humbling experience. Ego diminishes. My will does not rule. You give me the tenacity and the discipline to fight for and accomplish the destiny You've already sculpted for my soul.

Make that move, dear God, and lead me into the morning when You and I can ultimately tie that knot and be partners for life.

God:

It occurs to me that I've been looking for You in magnificent ways. For some time, I remember thinking that I would believe in You if you gave me certain signs, if You made Your appearance with a theatrical gesture that would render me senseless.

The terms and conditions I set for proof of Your existence, of course, were consistent with the psychological structure of who I am. I have, for a long time, refrained from living in the present, always concerned with the future, and always concerned with the grandness of the future. The future was real only if living in the present were preparation for a heroic and magnanimous future.

It was natural that I would only accept You if you appeared in a grand way. Isn't that the same term I have set for personal relationships? I can only accept people if I rewrite them by making them into something dramatic, heroic, and magnificent.

And why is this?

I cannot lie anymore with false testimonies about shared values; that I see in such people a reflection of the deepest sense of who I am, and that through them I wish to hold up living proof that such values exist outside myself, or that doing so relieves me of loneliness. The truth is that I have inflated those around me to compensate for the self I lack.

Isn't this why I have been sourly disappointed in so many of my relationships with my fellow human beings? Where am I going with all of this, Father? Well, I guess I am saying that it was only when I learned to see Your presence in the mundane, and, most of all, in the unforeseen aspects of my life that I felt Your presence. Too many small chance occurrences that impacted my life in significant ways occurred for me to pass them off as mere coincidences, or to interpret them in abstract expressions like, "gifts from the universe," "good karma." But then I wondered: Why is it that if You are so great that You chose to appear in the guise of the ordinary and the inconspicuous?

Could it be again that as our supreme moral teacher, Your small gestures are introductions into teaching us how to be humble? If one so great as Yourself can appear in such small ways, then it is indeed a comic sight when I, (we) need the bugles and trumpets and fanfare to announce our presence and to make our entrance into life which we do in many ways: our titles, our bloated stories, our class, our wealth. But didn't Your only Son appear in the shape of a child in the most inconspicuous way: poor and in a manger with smelly animals? How You shame us when we choose to live the reflective and contemplative life and honestly admit the results.

In appearing to me in such small ways, You force me to live in the present and to pay closer attention to the world and to the Now. Perhaps it is because I am too bent on conquering it that I often fail to feel connected to it.

But thank You, God, for the small ways you choose to appear in my life. Thank You for lovingly stamping me with the imprimatur of Your signature that reads: *storyteller*. Perhaps we all have to take note of the inconspicuous ways You make your presence felt, the little gifts you give us that lead to greater fortunes. We have to take all of these and interpret them and weave a narrative and tell a particular story. And, the story is an ode to You, and a self-revelation to us.

You and the material You give us to weave these narrative tapestries are the psychological passkeys we need to delve into our own souls and discover the buried little chips of light buried under debris that people-drifters leave as they make their way in and out of our lives.

Thank you, God, for the material that thickens your life-plot that builds and strengthens my life.

You are there, aren't You?

You are there, indeed.

Help me, Beloved Sentinel, whose presence I fear and want and do not want because I am terrified that it will vanish like all things I have associated with desiring. Help me to interpret the narratives correctly. Help me not to impose my hopes, my ego, my neuroses, and my fantasies on them. But instead, help me to create the desire to be persistently honest and give me clarity of insight to see the narratives as they are, and to see You in all of them.

God, I implore You to imbue me with the courage to be vulnerable and to open my heart fully, for you to take Your seat in my soul where I have hungered for You all my life.

My Dearest God:

I keep filling my heart with everything but You. I fill it with dreams and with other people, with their hopes, their sorrows, and their joys too. I fill it with the intensity of my will. I fill it with achievement and the glory of my own visions. Yet always, at the end of the quest, I am still left empty. I am still left with a bleeding, gaping heart whose dripping arteries yearn for pain relief.

I am still left with a hollow void and a scraped out feeling in my stomach, like a gutted fish. And always, my God, even when I struggled against You, and even when I denied You, always I have felt that it would take You and only You to fill that void.

I was born with a taste for Your plenitude. And I made the choice to free my soul from it because I wanted my freedom. I did not want to be enslaved by You and Your rules, and Your will. Dear God, that will that I lived in terror of, and still do.

What is a supplicant doing in the body of a human being and how can anyone desire to succumb to the will of God? I wondered. What if God should wish that I spend my life at the base of a garbage heap? What if His will and His vision for my life are at odds with the one I have crafted for myself? What if? What if? Those questions and their myriad possible answers have been the catalyst for many novels and beautiful films. But they have also driven me personally away from You. How could I ever know Your will? Would I want to know it? Deeply, deeply know it and give all of my life to it as a condition for happiness and peace?

God:

I do need to know Your will. I need to feel it pressing against my chest at night. I need it imprinted in the neurons of my brain. I need it because, God, I am exhausted by my own will. Not that it has not satisfied me at times. But it has also burdened me, and who knows, it may have even cost me a bit of my humanity. It is, at this point in my life, driving me to the brink of craziness. The anxiety and panic attacks, the excruciating migraine headaches, the cramps—are these nothing more than the burdens of my own ambitions? And the fantasies I have of walking on a beach with a dog and doing nothing? Is it from the tyranny of my own ambitions that I seek to escape? But those ambitions are what give my life purpose and meaning. From them I derive my identity.

Is it worth it? Answer me please. Is it worth it? Are the recovery and the ongoing construction of my humanity really Your will? Those who know You well, say resoundingly: Yes. But I need to know for myself. I need Your personal answer. I need Your loving whispers and Your reassurance. I can't find reassurance in other people's convictions and their faith, although I can find inspiration. I need a one-on-one conversation with You. I offer this letter as a plea.

Help me, dear God, to reconcile my will with Yours. Grant me the wisdom and the maturity to see the glory in this. The glory. The glory. Where is all the glory and how can I get it back? Should I be asking for glory? Please do not let me lose my humanity. Please don't.

Thank you, God. Thank You for giving it to me.

Lord:

What is faith to me? What does it mean in my life at this stage of my moral and spiritual development? I pose this question once more. I have been reading the expositions of some of Your brilliant spokesmen such as St. Augustine and St. Thomas Aquinas on the subject. I, however, have to find an explanation that resonates with me. One with which I am equally yoked.

I think that for me faith is belief in the rationality of Your will. Faith is the gift of realizing that there is logic to Your decisions and plans for my life even when I can't see them. It is the belief that nothing that is given to me can be detrimental to me regardless of how it appears to me.

Faith is *knowing* that my third eye will open: that part of my soul that can witness and discern the divine in the ordinary and the mundane. What they call the third eye is, I think, the spirit of discernment, our refined sense of proper perception that is part of our natural design.

Faith is seeing through the contingencies and finite nature of things on this earth, to recognize that my powers of interpretation and analysis cannot fully penetrate the providential plan You have carved for my life and the life of others. Faith is being grateful for whatever You give me, (that's going to be a very difficult one for me to accept). Ought I, therefore, to thank You for my horrible headaches? Well, I've had them since about the age of seven. Perhaps they will force me to acknowledge truths about my soul which I have not learned to comprehend. Perhaps they are guides to a higher way of existing. So, I say: Thank You for all that You have given me.

My Dearest God:

While I fought You and everything that You represent, I was still affirming You in some way. I have never ceased to really stand before You, have I?

What does it mean to be a militant atheist? What does it mean to be violently against the idea of God?

If You did not exist what would be the purpose of saying that one is violently against the non-existent? To carve out such a position for oneself is, in a sense, to invite psychological madness into one's life.

Think about it this way, God. If I saw a man slashing wildly though the air with a sword, and when queried about his actions he replied that he was fighting beasts that nobody could see, I would think of him as a lunatic fighting imaginary creatures. If there are no such creatures then all his muscular thrashings, heavy breathing, and overall expenditure of energy are foolish. Well, was I not that same crazy man? Here I was spending so many of my youthful years preaching against the idea of God, proclaiming with absolute rectitude that the concept *itself* had to be defeated, but more than that: The image of God that people carried within their hearts had to be annihilated. I saw myself as a super-being blessed and plagued with excess energy that needed a monster of a task to satiate that energy.

To be a true atheist, though, is to be indifferent to the idea of God. Those of us who do not believe in five-winged creatures and inch-long elves do not spend our lives fighting against the idea of them.

So I was that foolish man, ensnaring myself in self-deception, calling myself an enlightened atheist while fighting against something I claimed not to believe in.

My God, You are inescapable. You are all around us. Your presence saturates our thoughts and our lives. Even in denying You and fighting You I lay prostrate before You, helpless before the awesome spectacle of Your grandeur. It was a terror to behold because I was afraid that I would be lost in it, lost in the anonymity of amorphous space that swallows without recognition and without discrimination. And so, rather than carve a space for myself in that space which is You, I retreated and carved a space in the name of my immutable mind, my self-made soul. Jealous of the adulation and the praise heaped on You, I have spent my life killing the Father which You are in order to claim a conquest I thought was rightfully mine.

What madness, my God, what madness. Is it too late? Can I find my way back into Your loving embrace? Can I feel Your warmth enveloping me at night when I struggle against sleep because of the dreams and nightmares that plague my troubled soul, and more often than not, because I am also awakened by my own screams and shouts?

Do I have a right to You? Dare I call You my own? And what if You answer?

"Yes, Jason, I will take you back. You are forgiven for whatever it is that you think you have done and for all that I know you have done. And you will be loved despite the future wrongs you will commit as you and all others struggle in the name of your humanity."

What if my jealous and envious streak rises up? Few might admit to *God envy*. But it exists unconsciously in the psyche of all high achievers in one form or another.

What if my possessiveness clouds my moral character to the point where I increasingly despise Your other children? What if I want to see myself as Your favorite, what will happen? Will my fragile faith wither away knowing that none of Your children have a right to such a claim?

I know that my idiosyncrasies and my infantile yearnings do not constitute a legitimate mortgage on Your magnanimity.

I know these things and still, I desire. I yearn. I want. I need.

I need Your reassurance of things I have no right to demand.

I am only a child, God—morally, spiritually, intellectually. And in this strange way, because much of my youth was spent denying Your love and refusing Your grace, I want now to remain a child in order to relive my youth and recapture the bliss of what it must have felt for the child to be first embraced by the Father he refused to know.

God:

I rejected You. It is true. My anger was the one constant that cushioned my loneliness.

You took my father away from me. He came to me as a child and said: "I am repudiating you, your brother, and my entire family. God has called me out to be his servant. Observe, child, I am now married to Jesus whom I now love more than anything or anyone else in the world, even you, beloved, son, my precious first born."

I was 12 years old, and he was my best friend. Is he crazy? Has he been appointed by You to do Your work? Is Your will indelibly stamped in his mind in the form of this thing he calls a vision? And, is this vision, this inward mark of identity, responsible for what we call, sickness unto death? Is it an unrelenting despair whose relief can only be found in Your grace and love?

God, I do not know when or if I shall see him again. On my last visit to him in his cottage in the lush Blue Mountains of Jamaica over a decade ago, I can still see him kneeling in the middle of the dirt road as I drove away. His head was thrown back. He was looking up at the sky. His arms were raised to heaven and tears were streaming down his face. And over and over again he was thanking You for bringing me back. "Thank You. You, Sweet God, for delivering my first born back into my arms."

I was looking in the rearview mirror of my aunt's car. I stopped and contemplated the possibility of running back and throwing my arms around his neck and telling him that I loved him. But I decided not to do so. I have steeled myself against a lifetime of rejection. In the few hours we spent together he did not understand how we missed him and longed for him. He'd leave us again, he said. That's how he built the souls of his sons into soldiers, warriors for God. His arms were still outstretched, and he looked as if he was falling into a trance. I could not go back. I pressed the gas pedal and accelerated quickly, and I vowed never to see him again and never to return to the country in which I was born.

Oh, God, wherever You sit aloft looking down at all of us, bless him and all the afflicted—those we punish, and ridicule and cast aside and label as crazy. Bless them and bless the potential craziness that all of us carry in our minds. Give us strength to hold ourselves in dignity should we find ourselves the objects of shame and scorn. Let my back be as straight and upright, and my face as proud and healthy as my father's should I be as mocked and scorned as he has been all his life.

He says You speak to him, God; that You alone understand him; that Yours is the only unmediated voice that requires no interpretation. Deliver these words on my behalf to him, dear God. Tell him they are from his first born and that they are, for better or for worse, the only way I know how to honor him at this time:

Papa

I look upon your wrinkled brow in that

Space where Reason and Madness brew and come

To a stalemate,

Where your 3rd Eye grew, and then,

Swallowed up your youth and those who tasted your bad secrets,

Nightmares and saw your fallen angels with daggers for teeth who

Then became your friends.

•

Papa,

Many times,

That centered spot became my rocking chair,

My sail-away canoe I go tripping on when I can't get out of my own way.

And, caught between those furry brows,

I thought it better to be infected by your maddening spores

Than left here to grow old, and die alone.

Papa,

You ripped a thousand holes in my soul, and all

The books of the world can never fill them.

In my dream, one sparkle from those inhuman mountain lion eyes

Strikes me lightening hot.

And, like a fomenting many-holed pancake in a buttered skillet,

I am flipped, flattened out, and pressed

Against myself.

Lord:

There is a daily battle waged in my soul and in the souls of many of Your children. It is the battle between the public and the private self. We don so many masks and dramatize a plethora of personalities. We live fragmented lives in compartmentalized emotional zones.

I am the son of a woman and in that role I must dramatize the words uttered to my mother. I must be wary of maintaining the image of her son that she holds dear to her heart. I must hide my fragility from her because she will worry. If she worries, I experience guilt. Even when she detects my vulnerability, I sometimes have to deflect it and assuage her fears with manufactured bravery.

I am the professor in a class with students who thrill me one day and enrage me the next. Classroom decorum and professional protocol prevent me from bonding in spontaneous ways, a gesture here, a word there, a thought that rises up and then swells in my brain, a thought that could be underscored by a personal anecdote that might emotionally cement itself in a student's soul if at that moment, I spontaneously placed my hand on the hunched shoulder in the corner of the room as I am pacing. There are myriad ways to communicate ideas and yet, I am bound by the institutionalized logic of a particular style that professional teachers accept, as if there is a one-size-fits-all approach to ideas and their application to one's subjectivity—the edifice in one's soul beneath mind, thoughts, language, and public persona. The poetic element in my soul dies and I leave the classroom feeling like an inanimate cog in a huge efficient wheel that spins and spins but cannot differentiate itself from any other object in the world. This is what it means to be unanchored, to have a brain encased in flesh, to be suspended in a void—to be just out there, moving forward, hurtling like a train heading towards a future, but to still feel like I am going nowhere.

Ways of being are closed off.

I am friends with Paul, Nevada, Mary, Judith, Jose, and my brother. In each role I am a different person. But some may say, the personality springs from a single source—the heart of Jason; the heart of anyone who recognizes himself or herself in what I am saying. True. But can the core of one's soul speak its own truth despite the plethora of voices we force it to speak in? And if it can, will it sound like a foreign language to our ears? Sometimes I want to speak to everybody from that single core. In its own inimitable voice. Isn't that what we mean by integrity? Can the soul survive all the fragmented ways of existing that we impose upon it? Or is the soul naturally diverse, longing to express itself in the creative imagination of its inhabitants?

Do animals bring us comfort because with them we can simply be?

Truth be told, I sometimes feel like I'm being driven to craziness by the ephemeral nature of personal desires. But that is the price of loneliness borne out of metaphysical separation-anxiety that I chose when I abandoned You. The ephemeral and the non-everlasting are the path to unregulated freedom. But a self that is free is also, paradoxically, one that must be tethered to an indestructible foundation. When I gave You up philosophy became my religion. But it was not enough. Still, it is not enough. Philosophy, among other things, purports to solve the mysteries of human existence. To embrace the mysterious and affirm life while engaging in the enterprise of philosophy is to act the fool—some would say.

Why can't I simply have the courage to listen? Why do I pollute my center of gravity with the expectations of others? Why do I internalize their prejudices, their weaknesses, and their neuroses as my own? Even worse: why, in those moments when I feel unworthy of the deepest love of others, do I wear new false masks in order to ward them off? Now that's hubris, isn't it? To imagine that I'm so powerful that I have to warn others about myself?

It is the poison inside of me that I am afraid of. And realizing the allure that allegedly mysterious and dangerous people hold over others, I seek to attract others under false pretense of repelling them so that they may help me extract the poison. It all comes back to the same form of spiritual cannibalism, doesn't it? Gorging on the spirit of others so they may extract the poisons lodged inside of me, toxins that prevent me from feeling fully fed.

Perhaps You might say that this is not madness. It is human. Perhaps You might say:

"Such are the ways of your humanity. These are the mazes through which you must navigate your life journey, and it is only by facing them and acknowledging them that you can negotiate your own humanity and transform it into something closer to the Divine."

No short cuts are there? No easy way to exaltation and spiritual ecstasy. My condemnation of the fragmented lives we live and my frustration over the masks we wear are ways of being in the world.

I want moral coherence. I am tired of living a morally fragmented life, carving up my humanity, like my heart, into tiny pieces of hors d'oeuvres and feeding them to uninvited guests whom I cannot refuse. And who cannot see me. I walk in shame, Lord. But not disgraced, not fully ruined like the dead fetus lying in his ruined salt in his mother's sack.

And if I should begin the process of ripping the masks away, will You reveal Your face to me? Will I see and feel You in the center of my core? Are You there, my God? If You are not, then how can I live without the masks, the personalities, and the elegantly crafted images I have worn to trick, control, manipulate and yet, also, to love the world with? Those are the currencies I use along with the intellect, the bright smile, and conflicted heart You have given me to wander through this world. If I give them up because they wear down my soul and because they fail to purchase the happiness I had hoped for, will Your presence be enough? Can Your non-complicated love satisfy a void that has grown bigger with each passing year? Is Your love a simple love?

God:

The philosopher Jacob Needleman says that "Our culture has generally tended to solve its problems without experiencing its questions." This is one of the reasons why I have found refuge in philosophy. I can attempt to solve questions without experiencing them emotionally. It is the reason philosophy can neither take the place of You, nor the religion I abandoned. Philosophy is a form of self-defense sprung from a life of repressed hatred. When You were there, You were rooted in my heart among the multitude of arteries. You were there. Naturally. Peacefully.

In violence I tore You out. And what took its place had to be justified. It had to be rational. Something leapt up instinctually to take Your place. Some new myth was created to justify the murder committed against You. So, I created a fable about a poisonous womb and a trapped fetus suffocating in gaseous fumes. This child was looking for Father. He was looking for Daddy in the Poisonous Womb. And he asked: What is it that makes this womb so poisonous? The growing vegetable that ought not be a vegetable but a blessed fruit? Or the baby vampire that takes away life slowly as the absence of breaking dawn keeps him from coming into being?

Vengeance is mine! Breathed the first fetus.

And then,

It became the word of God.

And I was born.

You were dead.

And I thought: I have found freedom.

Now what I thought was freedom tastes ominously like death.

Forgive me.

Rearranging the words of my forlorn poetess: A row of headstones separates me from You. And from where I stand, I simply cannot see where there is to get to.

I, we, all of us who call ourselves deep thinkers ponder the questions of life intellectually, but we never penetrate them with the intrusive messiness of our emotional lives. Well, God, in this forum with you, in my attempt to speak with you one on one, I am allaying the protocols of the professional life and trying to experience my questions with You.

If we live lives unrelated to our deepest questions then either our answers will be trite and glib—manufactured according to the "spiritual and emotional needs" of our particular era—or we will not even recognize the answers when they come to us in surprising ways. Obsessed with getting immediate answers, we ignore questions that lead to more questions and then some. We ignore questions that will lead by means of the uncertainty of their answers. Answers that, nevertheless, will inspire us to continue searching for more answers that might teach us lessons we find distasteful.

God, that is what being a perpetual child is like, isn't it? Not having the courage to accept answers that disappoint initially but that ultimately liberate and transform. Like the eternal child, I want the answers to satisfy a need I have now, and I want it now.

Lord, please take my hand and give me the strength to make the journey from childhood into spiritual adulthood.

Give me the courage to accept those answers that may disappoint, and the faith to accept the eternal goodness of who You are. Grant me the unflinching rectitude of standing firm in this belief: No answer that You grant to me can ever be futile or irrelevant in the context of the life that You gave me.

Grant me this, God, not that my life might be happier, but that I may grow closer into the image of what You intend me to be.

Dear God:

I have been thinking about the issue of *lack,* (existentialist philosophers have called it *exigency*) that seems to be a permanent feature in the human soul today. I have been wondering: Why is it that in a society such as ours in which we fill our lives with experiences and actions, loneliness is stubbornly pervasive?

I realize that we could rid ourselves of the cultural symbols and material goods—soul-killing clutter—that our culture has told us are the pre-requisites for a good life; the social goods that have meandered into our personal space. Then the question arises: How does one live in a world in which such trivial goods are conditions for a sense of survival?

All right, I could say that we should strive to wean ourselves from those false values. In You are to be found the highest values.

Is it true, however, that this lack, this soul vacancy, is merely an existential symptom of our self-imposed exile from You? Or let me ask You this: Did You hardwire us for such a lack? I remember as far back as the age of three, feeling this loneliness. I would straddle that old rusty fence on my grandfather's beach home in Yallas, Jamaica, and stare out at the ocean and feel deep metaphysical loneliness. I would feel the vastness of the ocean and experience incompleteness in the center of my soul. Psychologists would say I was simply missing my parents who were away for too long. Perhaps, but to a child what difference does it make?

This is why I resented You for many years. I felt that You left out a piece of my soul. You put me here on this earth as an unfinished specimen and then left the burden of filling up that soul to me. But what on earth did I do to deserve this? What has a child done to deserve this? Some are born with missing limbs or mal-functioning organs, but that a three-year-old child felt that he was born with a piece of his soul missing, or that he was born with a void in the soul that he'd been given—I want to fathom it. I remember wondering in later childhood if there had been a twin who'd shared my mother's womb with me and, if in the midst of our amniotic playful jousting, he or she had been ripped away from my embrace. Was it this separation that had caused me to feel such devastating loneliness as soon as I was able to perceive myself as a separate entity from the objects in the world around me?

Why plant this void in us, God? Why give us this terrible inborn anguish? What purpose does it serve? Is that the foundation of our instinctual life? Is that the source of the religious impulse? Some say that even if You did not exist we would have invented You because of the great unexplainable longing and yearning with which we come into the world. Our mother's milk is not enough, the love from family is insufficient, the endless playmates—and in my case, the inability to bond with playmates, as if something in me sensed that they would never be enough, that they would only gingerly satiate a hunger that knew no end and thereby open up an omnivorous appetite that would swallow up my whole existence—were never enough.

You put this in me, God, and now what? Now what? Where does it all lead and when does it end? When does it end? Does it ever end?

God:

I am thinking about the meaning of moral *becoming*. Perhaps it is obsession with becoming that will end the incompleteness in my soul. Is the fundamental lack at the core of my existence truly the same for everyone else?

How does a mother deal with lack when she realizes that her own children have failed to fill her up in the way she had imagined? How does a woman deal with lack, or the world for that matter, after she confesses to You one night in a moment of radical honesty, the following: "Motherhood has left me more depleted than fulfilled. If I had to do it over again, I would not have had children. I wish my children knew this so guilt would drive them to spend their lives serving me."

Perhaps there are irreconcilable states of tension that plague the human condition and all we can do is embrace the mystery and affirm life and the living.

How to become? This is the fundamental issue of my 21st century. What to become? The traditional foundations, the fixed and immutable truths have been eroded by science, reason, and that strange, strange concept known as progress. Few of us can ever go back. We know too much. We are critically educated and trained to question much of what we have been taught are Your laws and Your ways. Do you think I'm going to "dumb down my mind" I want to say, to fit into Your design just to be make myself happy?

I wish I could.

I deeply want to.

Sometimes need is belief.

Sometimes need is so paralyzing belief is not possible. This is what I sometimes feel although some writer once wrote something on the order of: "Men who don't believe in God, don't believe in nothing. Rather they believe in anything."

Belief is unseated from its high chair when one believes in anything. Indiscriminate belief in anything is spiritual anarchy, is it not? Mental nihilism that collapses into the absurdity of belief in everything.

So, You have placed this pervasive inescapable sense of lack in my soul, and I am toying with the idea that this is a way for me to get to You. But You placed it there even before I rejected You, for as a child I spoke with You, served as an altar boy and often felt close to You. Okay, maybe You knew that I would be driven from You by the power of my own maniacal will. I feel this lack and I seek to make my life over by crafting a vision of the person I wish to become. This portrait will contain the features that the original soul You gave me lacked.

You know the story, God. You know it well. You have always known it. One day it hit me in the form of an informed and unsolicited piece of knowing that it would require a great return to You for this incompleteness to be made whole.

This *knowing* I received abstractly without any emotional feelings. I thought: *This is silly. I have no feeling for the concept of a God, and even if He does exist, I would not know how to go about knowing Him.*

But this abstract knowledge planted itself in my mind. I began to feel religious impulses. Overpowering urges to enter a church at 2 a.m. in the morning; urges to speak Your name while doubting and then denying Your existence, and laughing at myself in embarrassment; feeling like both an intellectual fraud and a weakling for comporting myself in such a weak and pathetic way when weeping in awe when looking at the iconography of the Church, feeling weak in the knees while gazing up at the bleeding St. Sebastian, and yet, still proclaiming myself a proud and rational atheist. At least I had had the good grace to relinquish the sobriquet militant atheist. I was losing, I later realized, some of my desperation and hysteria over You.

You called me, didn't you? First by the mind and then the call's cry found the heart. But my heart heeded the call not from a harmonious reconciliation with the mind. My heart was driven by sheer desperation and sheer boredom with suffering.

I told people: "I will not be at one with God. I want to be a servant of God, to do His work. I know this even though I know that I am not ready, even though I neither believe in Him nor trust Him entirely. I have no emotional relationship with Him." And some of them could not understand how a cerebral man whose principled avowed advocacy of reason had caused him to once break with those he deemed mindless irrationalists could speak in such a manner. I could not explain it to myself—as you well know—much less to them. In moments of lightheartedness, I would say: "Embrace the mystery and affirm existence nevertheless."

There is a time, however, when the soul struggles to mend itself despite the will that governs it. It struggles, and its destiny becomes apparent. It begins to see You God, in the form of your messengers and in Your "small acts." A discerning and wise mind eventually accepts the fact that it can no longer dismiss phenomena as just random acts of nature. Too many of the latter point to a substantial pattern. Several patterns point to an ordered and orchestrated intelligence. It is that simple to me now. It just is.

One wills to embrace the mystery and affirm existence and slowly, over time, the willing ceases. One is inseparable from the mystery.

An ordered moral becoming.

This is my mantra.

It has to lead to You. This is the path that carves its way through the bankruptcy of my tired soul, the path that, out of necessity, makes a straight and desperate dash to You. I carve that path each day. When doubt overtakes my mind an act of will guides the path.

I nurture that path even when I think: *Jason, you're an idiot. He is not there. This is only your psychological weakness: false humility. Write and sing a glorious hymn in your own voice. Rise by your own grace and strength in the name of the potential best within you.*

I continue to carve that path out of sheer willpower.

I doubt.

I doubt.

I grow weary of not hearing Your voice and feeling like I am left alone in the wilderness.

Still, I nurture that path. Hopeful that I can trod its highway one day.

And that is faith. That is faith, isn't it? I am trying to make my own faith with the raw material of my soul. I am finding, in my way, what faith is; establishing a relationship to that concept that has been talked about for ages. But it is something that has to be cultivated, acquired, and known by each person himself. The lack, the deep exigency, and the pervasive loneliness are the catalysts that propel me into your reach.

You made me incomplete so that I may have the honor of struggling to discover what a holy act of creation looks like.

Day by day, humbly, I wait to see the unfolding of my faith.

I listen.

I strain.

I listen.

And at last, I am learning to take in not just the exalted and tortured symphonies, the heroic trumpets, but the small whispers, the "small acts," the faintest of voices in the sweetest of tones. Your voice comes in many forms. How does a man accustomed to hearing only the gargantuan and the tumultuous sirens accompanying glorious achievements or idealistic visionary dreams re-train his ear to hear Your whispery voice amidst the cacophony of modern life?

You give us all, You give me, a glimpse of what it is like to be a creator. You, for whom I feel much love now as you fill me with inspiration and Divine Insight. You have made me a participant in your creation by showing me how the lack and the void need not lead to desperation. Through your invisible hand guiding a child to take his first steps, You make me realize that I must earn some portion not of your love, but of your respect.

By what right do I demand that You should have filled my soul to the brim from birth? Why indeed should You have given me everything? Isn't that what we call spoiling children? As our parents and teachers instruct us in how to become wage earners so that we can support ourselves—rather than giving us all the material resources for our survival—so You, benevolent God, have given me my void and my despised loneliness with the intention of showing me what it really takes to build my own life, to create an edifice and a mansion within myself. As I have glorified and deified and given God-like status to achievements and glory, the acquisitions and the respect of friends, the fame of others and the intimidation and defeat of my adversaries, You have shown me again, slowly and painfully, the ephemeral, the emptiness of those values when they are not tethered to an unshakeable foundation. Behind them lies the abyss—constant, unchanging, and enveloping in its blinding darkness—where indiscriminate freedom is free to reign.

God:

My God, my God. I have bled my soul to death with thousands of tiny scratches. Some kill theirs with swift blows. Others starve theirs to death by never acknowledging that they have one. Have I already said this before?

And why is it that tomorrow or, perhaps, in a few days I will go on bleeding that soul in many ways? Experts will say it is because my subconscious has been habituated to behave in certain ways and that psychological bad habits are difficult to break.

So, here is my prayer to You, God.

I won't ask for a bloodless soul.

I won't ask for it because I realize that if I am ever to become a spiritual adult in this world, then I have a responsibility to stop being an accessory to the murder of my spirit.

Socrates was correct. The only harm that comes to a good man is the harm that he inflicts on himself. Only we can sully and dirty our spirits.

I won't ask You to steer me from every situation that might sully this soul because I don't want to be spared the responsibility of cleaning up my own mess, of learning to nurture that which You gave me, and that which was pure when it inhabited my body in my mother's womb. If You do all these for me, God, then, indeed, I shall remain a child forever and will never learn how to discipline my own will against the damage I do to myself.

I pray, Lord, that You will grant me the insight to know that each scratch I inflict against my soul can ultimately be cured only by seeking the bliss of your protection and the amazing grace of your limitless love.

I pray that every self-infraction against my soul also comes with the reminder of the Herculean efforts I will have to pursue to find my rightful place by Your side.

I pray that each time I rebel against the nature of my divine soul that I have the integrity not to deceive myself into thinking that there are shortcuts back to the path I trod, and that You have paved.

I pray that in those hardened times when the demands of my soul become too painful to hear, and my instincts turn me from the duty of repair, that I at least have the ear to distinguish between the cry of innocence and the howl of despair, and to know that with You, all sorrowful moans can be transformed into symphonic cries of jubilation.

I pray that in those irascible moments when I am tempted to do damage to myself, that the tearful faces of my loved ones etch their likeness into my heart, and that I will have the compassion to read the disappointment and devastation in their eyes, to see the holy sacrifices they have made, and to know that they never asked for anything in return but my simple happiness.

I pray, my benevolent life-giver, that You oversee my life and not spare me all my foolish mistakes but grant me the patience to learn from the mistakes, to weave an intelligent narrative that I can use to interpret my life. Grant me the power of insight to maintain a vigilant eye upon my own soul behavior. Guide me in doing all this with compassion rather than with condemnation.

I am not asking for miracles, nor am I pleading for free handouts. No special protection against the things that are in my power to determine do I ask for.

Strength and peace I seek.

Strength to become what know I ought to become.

Peace to be satisfied with the result.

Strength to be a good soldier.

Peace to be still and remain rooted in my convictions when exhaustion wears me down.

Grant me my requests!

I have asked for them in a spirit of fairness.

It is your companionship that I most desperately need.

Thank you, my God.

Thank you for granting me all that I have asked for in fairness.

God:

My story is a really the story of beating the odds isn't it? I always knew I wanted to be a writer. I was always well aware of the gift that you gave me. I nurtured it and I treasured it, but I never gave myself the gift of penmanship. I believe that I was writing in my head long before I learned how to write.

America.

The journey to America.

Didn't my father, that mad prognosticator, tell me a long time ago when I was still a child that my mother would take me and my brother to America? So, I came and decided on two careers: a novelist and a philosopher. And through all the struggles, the rejections, the relentless effort of putting myself through school, the money that never seemed to be enough, You gave me the strength to overcome every obstacle. You removed them. And now that I think of it, You obstructed my paths as I had carved them out according to my will. No, I guess You obstructed nothing. You arranged my life the way You designed it. And You strengthened me with the courage of my convictions to not be swayed from my vocation.

Thank You, my God, thank You for taking me on an incredible journey. At twenty I came to this country armed with nothing but dreams, $120 in my pocket, and the moral support of a loving family. That's plenty, I suppose. I came. I saw. I wanted nothing more than to achieve and make something of my life. And so, it is time to give back to You, except You have asked for nothing. But now is the time for gratitude and appreciation. I don't want You to think that I am an ungrateful miscreant. I am grateful, Lord, you know that now, don't You? I do thank You for giving me the life that I dreamed of, and the success I thought would never come, the success that comes in small doses and that provides the fuel for a spirit that did run dry.

Well, God, I have never thanked You for the small down payments. I have lived for the dream, often cursing the small victories as pitiful and meager means to those dreams. Thank You for all of them. They taught me the virtues of delayed gratification, struggle, and the ability to accept people and life experiences I regarded as beneath me. They taught me the skill of the spiritual bricklayer: the art of placing one brick at a time consciously, slowly, and with a view of the edifice in mind.

Where does perseverance come from? Where do stubbornness and the inability to take no for an answer originate? It seems, once more, like many of my traits already existed as seedlings in my soul from as far back as I can remember. And though they have haunted me, driven me to fatigue and tortured my soul, I feel like thanking You again.

Why?

Is this some masochistic attempt at redemption? Why the need to thank You for some of the things that have brought the most pain? It's not just me. The self-mortifiers do the same. And if we thank You for that which brings us pain, aren't we authoring invitations for greater afflictions?

Perhaps, once more, it all comes down to an issue of faith. We need to believe that we have to thank You, for it is better to be thankful for the inevitable than to resent it. Psychologically speaking God, we know that this makes more sense. It's like the person trapped in a hurricane zone who knows he can't get out, and who knows the impending storm will hit. Better for him to accept it and acclimatize himself psychically for the imminent. That way he won't be cynical and devastated when his hopes and aspirations are shattered.

We know that the complete eradication of pain and suffering on earth is impossible. Wisdom and experience inform us that no one—not even Jesus—was spared agony. Thanking You for them is my way, I think, of imbuing them with status. Holy unwanted obstacles might be better than orchestrated pleasures because the force of the holy and unwanted challenges pushes us outside our zones of comfort. They force us to recreate ourselves.

How much quicker do rural folks recover from natural disasters that destroy their farms and livelihood than yuppies who "mess up" their lives through vices of character. My challenges have forced me to seek those new areas of adaptations that are central to soul maturation. Some call it evolutionary consciousness. Left to my own devices would I have propelled myself to such heights?

And so, I thank You not for the challenges that are inevitable, not for the pragmatic part of me that thinks it is wiser to give thanks for something I'll receive whether I want it or not. But I also know that we ought never to tell the gift-giver what we want as a gift or set the conditions for receiving a gift. I feel this is what You are flooding my thoughts with at this very moment. We have to be free to receive Your gifts in whatever form they appear. On first appearance, those gifts sometimes seem like manna from heaven. Other gifts seem like plagues. We resent them. They spoil our plans.

Give me faith, God, to ask You to shower me with Your gifts but without the temptation to corrupt myself by setting the terms of Your gifts in my requests.

Grant me, God, the faith to believe that none of Your gifts can ever be bad for me because of the essence of what I am.

Illuminate my mind so I may know that a gift perceived as irrelevant to my material desires is a gift in disguise for my future *soul-self*, a gift that You will eventually deliver to me on the day that I have earned it.

Bless me with the conviction to joyously say on my deathbed: "Thank God You disappointed me then, for now I see how authentic my life turned out to be."

I ask for trust, God. Trust in the inherent benevolence of You—the ultimate gift-giver.

And I should learn to completely trust You again, then I may learn to trust my fellow humans in a deeper way.

May I learn to trust their capacity to offer me the gifts of their souls and leave them free to love me in the ways they know how to love.

In so doing, I will have granted them their freedom, and I will have loved them in the deepest humanly possible way: a small version of the way they are loved by You.

God:

I'd like to continue this letter on gift-giving and on seeing You as the ultimate gift-giver. I began by thanking You for making my immigrant dreams come true. Now I am rambling on about something else. You are inspiring me, leading my fingers to type words I didn't plan.

All right, You gift-giver. I want more than anything to allow people the freedom to love me in ways natural for them. I am, admittedly, responsible for much of my unhappiness because I set the terms for how I wish to be loved. Those terms are determined by my needs. Always, my needs. Those needs eat at my soul. They are born of deprivation and fears of abandonment. I have used them as emotional coercers, manipulating people into loving me the way I need to be loved; loving me in ways that are incompatible with who they are.

Somewhere I got lost. No. Actually, it's more than being lost. Somewhere I lost my relationship to You. That loss was accompanied by a great tragedy: the inability to believe in the gift-giver. A boy in my high school once remarked that God was like Santa Claus. One outgrew him eventually. I still believed in You then and I remembered being struck by the analogy between God and Santa Claus. I had not made an association with the gift-giver. But if what he said was true, then he was identifying a trait in us that undermines the capacity for unlimited kindness and compassion.

Is the image of You as the gift-giver being irrevocably lost today? Is that why Christmas seems increasingly like a frantic rush to fill our own voids? The more gifts I give the more I can anticipate not just receiving but filling a void in people's life. This desire supersedes the desire to give from a spirit that gives because by nature it is gift-giving. *The unconscious agitation in the pursuit of giving becomes a substitute for the pure and simple joy of giving.*

If I learned how to see You again as the ultimate gift-giver, then perhaps my demands for love would be less tyrannical, and the conditions under which I offer my love would not be so harsh. If I truly see You as the gift-giver, and I incorporate

You into my heart, then I become like an overflowing cup that gives without thought, without want, without doubt. I give from an overabundant nature. This plenitude is You.

This is what I desire. So how do I ask for this, God? I am trying to ask You for things that will help me to grow. I don't wish for free rides from You.

No. I'm lying.

Of course, I want free rides.

But I'm trying to rid myself of the desire to demand free rides. If I do not, I shall never be weaned from my insecurities and pettiness. So again, help me formulate this demand, God. Help me learn how to pray for this in a way that will make You proud of me and make me whole.

It boils down to a plea: help me to learn to trust You again. I don't know how You'll do that. Perhaps my trust in my fellow human beings will grow stronger, and You will use them as conduits for my moral training. But I do know that the image of You as the eternal and benevolent gift-giver can only return after I learn to trust.

I want that trust back, God. I really do.

I need to see You as the gift-giver. I know that I need to see You as the gift-giver because my father never gave me a gift. Not once. No birthday presents, no Christmas presents. His only gifts were hugs, kisses, sweet words, his songs and his endless tears. Perhaps I should have been satisfied with them. I was not.

I need to see you as the gift-giver because for years I saw You as a thief. You were the bogeyman who stole my father—the first friend I ever made and loved, my best friend in the whole world. You took him as one of Your soldiers who had to go to war for Your crusade.

I need to see You as the gift-giver because You have been my greatest competitor—the giant jaw that stands ready to swallow the pleasures I concoct to ameliorate the pains of privation.

But can I disown those human reasons when they are the only things I have right now with which to reach You? Can I loftily embrace the part of You in me I want to embrace when I have yet to reconstruct and expand the humanity You endowed me with? Need the two be mutually exclusive?

From where I stand, I simply cannot see where there is to get to.

It's late, God. I have to teach tomorrow, and I am tired. I'd like to continue to write to You throughout the night, but then, would I have the stamina to teach? You know, I think very soon I'm going to pull one of those "all nighters." Just the two of us.

"My date with God," I'll call it, and see what the hangover feels like. I can imagine myself saying to my class: Guess what? I've got a hangover from my date with God. I'd probably be arrested God, and then I would have to thank You for that and then see that as a gift. Do You see what happens when a pen is led to write things the heart desperately wishes for but the mind rejects?

It's been fun, Lord, a lot of fun. Thank You for the questions You wrote into my heart and the inspiration to deal with them head-on. The philosopher's point that our culture has generally tended to solve its problems without experiencing its questions haunts me again. I've opened up my heart and asked You a lot of questions. Thank You for experiencing them with me. Looking forward to our all-night date.

God:

I went to bed in such a glorious mood thanking You for making all my immigrant dreams come true. And then, I was awakened this morning by a friend telling me that this West African immigrant was gunned down in his apartment by four police officers who, having suspected him of rape, emptied their guns on him through his apartment doors and walls. He was a newly minted immigrant. He was not arrested. He was not questioned. They shot and killed him, emptying forty-two bullets inside of him. He was defenseless. It turns out he was innocent. Was that Your gift to him? How in hell, pardon my irreverence, was that in his highest good? While I was waxing philosophical and spiritual with You in my safe apartment, in my safe neighborhood, a man was gunned down brutally while my love odes to You were pouring out.

From where I now sit, I simply cannot see how to go on. Is there a place to get to?

What is going on in this world? Now a great anger and bitterness is swelling up inside of me like a vampire threatening to devour an authentic soul I am trying to cultivate.

When is all this sport killing going to stop? A few weeks ago, a young black girl called 911 for assistance. On arrival at the scene, the police emptied nine bullets into her car. She was unarmed. She was frightened. Her car had broken down. Her potential saviors became her executioners.

That immigrant leaves parents behind. They are coming to collect his body. Where are his dreams now? Up there on Your lap? Like me, Lord he came. He saw. He dreamed that his life would be filled with meaning and, perhaps, some small sign from his New World that life is a value, and that he is a value. He left behind not just a family but a family of individuals with dreams. He carried to this land not just his dreams, but the dreams of those he left behind. Through him, they would live their lives vicariously, praying that their dreams might be realized through his life. His life could be a spectacle they could behold and contemplate.

His mother grieves. She weeps. It could have been my mother. It could have been any of our mothers.

Was it her only son?

My chest is tight. I am suffocating. I am to teach in thirty minutes. I am not prepared for my classes. The swelling in my chest is sucking the air out of me. Last night I went to bed filled with peace, looking forward to our date and now, and now what?

Now what?

Was he frightened when he heard the shouts in the hallway? As he lay dying did his homeland come to mind, and did the longing for his mother's arms and the desire to return to her womb fill him with peace or escalating fright?

Did he see Your face in his final gasp for air?

From where I stand, facing my window looking out at the city of St. Louis, I see more headstones separating you from me. And I simply cannot see where there is to get to.

These questions betray my emotions now, God. My heart is heavy, and I want to curl into the ball-like form of early life, back into my mother's womb and start life over. I want to come back as something different. Here then, is my renunciation of the Now. This is my rebellion, once more, against You.

Fill his family's heart with peace. And fill my heart, and the hearts of those who are terrified—not just of living, but of existence—with Your consoling love and the courage never to give up in our search for the practices of goodness and compassion.

And, for those who took his life dear God, it is with every idealistic fiber of my body that I ask this: Release them from the cycle of violence in which they are entrapped. In my efforts to demonize them and to call on You to punish them without mercy, I remember that they work the violent streets by day and by night. I remember that they encounter the face of evil much too often. I remember that they have become swallowed up by the violence they pledge to combat. I remember that they, too, are human beings and that as humans we all internalize the neuroses of others' prejudices, hatred, and fears. Some unleash that which they have internalized against themselves and self-destruct. Others turn against their families. And sometimes those who are sent to protect us turn against us.

Align them once more, God, to their ethical centers of gravity. Set their moral compasses straight and steer them back to their unknown goodness.

Let them see the face of goodness in their mothers and grandmothers, in the first unsure smile of an infant and in expressions of admiration on the faces of those they love. Renew their faith in the possibility and existence of goodness so that they might better know how to fight for a world in which goodness might prevail without destroying the preconditions for its very existence. Return to them their goodness. Do it as much for their sake as for the sake of all of us who need a glimpse of it to proceed with our lives.

I once heard a young, black American female sociologist tell a group of inner-city students the following: "Your goodness is never a guarantee that bad things will not happen to you. But your goodness is the only source from which you will heal from the bad things that will happen to you."

She was not preaching doom and gloom. Bad things happen to good people all the time. Suffering and struggle are a part of life. You should not walk around expecting to be afflicted at any moment. But when bad things happen you should not be shocked. No one is immune to misfortune.

Guide these words and the truth that they carry to my subconscious so that I become habituated to seek goodness, and to know that evil is impotent in its presence. Evil can destroy, but unlike goodness, it cannot create.

Let me believe in the goodness of the world and of people. In times of strife and grief, let me believe and say these words again and again: "My goodness is never a guarantee against bad things happening to me. But my goodness is my only source of recovering and healing from the bad things that will happen."

Lord, as I venture out into this world I sometimes perceive as terrifying, strengthen my moral center. Let my thoughts, my actions, and my wishes emanate from Your Divine Center. Replenish it, dear God, when it runs dry. You are its source. You are its sustainer. You give it life. Nourish it. I ask this of You, my unfailing God, in the name of all that You are, and in the name of all that You must continue to mean in my life and in the lives of those who need You and don't know it.

God:

What is happening to young people today? I have spent a lifetime preparing to be an educator. Now it is upsetting to be faced with their virulent apathy.

What's festering inside the hearts of young adults who come to a class to sleep, to be rude, and to show almost every emotion except enthusiasm for learning? Is it because their purpose for being in school is predominantly tied to a purely economic incentive? Do they think that any course that does not tangibly maximize their earning potential ought to so easily be dismissed?

Where is the hunger that I saw in students when I was growing up? Where is that earnestness of character that translates into a burning drive to make oneself into a better person by cultivating an ethos and a moral character from the values offered by one's education? I know sundry explanations are offered from time to time. But how does one begin to search even remotely for the root of this discontent? Are students sensing that something in general is terribly amiss? Are their lethargy and disengagement unconscious attempts to teach us something? How can I listen when I want to shout: "What is wrong with you all? You have an opportunity to make something of your lives, and here are some of you, throwing it away, snapping gum and rolling your eyes?"

Perhaps they have been abandoned in crucial ways and feel that attempts to guide them in the classroom are futile. Can abandoned people be guided? Guidance presupposes a sense of direction. They can't perceive direction because they have no concept of it. They have no direction because they have no sight. They cannot see because their eyes were never trained to focus on the long view, the view beyond the satisfaction of the wants and desires of the shallow, ephemeral present. If they have no sight, then they can have no vision. If they have no vision and no direction, then they have obliterated their sense of the future. If they have done this, then they have abandoned meaningful living. If they are not responsible for their lives, how can they be trusted with freedom and liberty?

They cannot thrive and flourish—hence their lethargy and disengagement. They make movements, but they are only that: mechanical motions. They believe in the futility of engagements. Engagement is risky participation in life projects.

One becomes a coparticipant in the creation of one's life. They feel they have nothing to participate in because there is no meaningful future to inherit. Given a multitude of particulars but nothing substantively concrete, they have an incomprehensible and mysterious want for something in general but nothing in particular. What is the root of that want that stems from a void they cannot name?

I, too, have returned to the void Lord, and it is my students who frustrate me and who shove me back into it. What a horrible void, like a dust-filled vacuum bag tied around my head, cutting off sight, hearing, smell, and breathing.

They have been taught that they are complete, that they come from the land of abundance; taught to equate fulfillment with the acquisition of every gadget, every coined idea that satisfies a manufactured need.

False needs are created for them where they do not exist in their hearts.

Real needs are ignored because their fulfillment requires the perseverance of a lover, the dedication of a saint, and the relentless discipline of a martyr.

Life as we know it needs to be deeply evaluated. Inchoate and panic-driven activities that temporarily fill these endless voids need to cease.

We need to be still. Oughtn't we to listen to the sobbing desperation of our souls and not just the pleas of our hearts, the immediate demands of our loins, and the acquisitiveness of our craven eyes?

But such is the nature of the world my students have inherited. Inundated with information about the value of things they are seduced into thinking they must acquire long before they have paid for it with their sweat and blood, they give up before experience even fails them. I sometimes think the first thought on their minds about any and every issue is: *What's the use?*

Should I give up on them? Should they be weeded out to make room for those whose hunger is real?

Fill them with hunger, God. And with desire for the fulfillment that they think is theirs by right. Let them learn to earn their soul-keep. Rid them of their automatic sense of entitlement and their self-centered obsession with their parochial "worlds." Let them spiritually feel a degree of hunger analogous to the hunger of starving children in remote lands. Inculcate in them permanence of commitment so that they may know that our humanity, the raw materials of which You gave us, is one that we must achieve collectively.

Dear God:

I've been thinking about how difficult it is for us to remove the cultural brandings that we wear that give us this sense of belonging and of being just like everyone else. What price do we pay for wearing those manufactured markers?

You give us inklings of other worlds and of moral possibilities so removed from the realities of our tawdry present. When we communicate them to others, they brand us as crackpots. It is strange when sickness takes on the sheen of normality and moral health appears pathological to those whose craziness has been granted societal legitimacy.

I know that to be moral is to be practical. I know because the price the soul pays when it fakes reality is existential death. The consequences are too great. It would be impractical to live a life in which the soul is pulled so heavily down by the gravity of our sins—impractical that is, if we wish to flourish rather than merely exist.

Carl Jung writes: "The visionary does not have a referent, a counterpart in reality." How can I find the strength to continue to believe in a world in which the values I most deeply believe in have not yet found their home?

I know, God, that there are spiritual heroes full of visions that You have sown in their souls. They are silent carriers of moral inoculants against the idea pathogens that suffuse our society. They sometimes, though, feel that there are no recipient hosts in which to implant the life-giving elixirs You have created within them. They are condemned to live in a world that cannot condone the essence of who they are. In our world we often call such people sick. Is that what my father is? Is he a sick man? Or is he one of Your blessed visionaries?

Give Your visionaries, God, the strength to carry on. Let them not despair in those moments when they feel they are living on a dead planet surrounded by customized deafness.

They are the benefactors of our world, God, and we need them to carry us to higher stages of civilization, to higher levels of consciousness; consciousness that can both mediate and transcend the shallow present in which we are mired. They are Your spiritual progenitors, Lord, and they entice us to awaken from our self-incurred moral laziness. They entreat us to take the same degree of sophistication that we apply to the natural world—conquering nature and mastering the brutish elements of physical life—and turn it inward with a view toward moral and spiritual advancement.

Isn't it about time that we unlearned the foibles that have despoiled our souls? We know how to distinguish poisonous mushrooms from nutritional ones. We know which chemicals are harmful to our bodies. We know how to predict when hurricanes are arriving, and how to inoculate ourselves from flesh-eating bacteria and other maladies of nature. And yet, we have not learned how to really apply and cultivate the rules for our soul nourishment.

The Danish philosopher Søren Kierkegaard wrote in the nineteenth century that we were living in lost quietness. He said we were indifferent to who we really were at the deepest core. We lived as if we were purely or mostly bodily creatures who could find satisfaction from physical, material, and sensuous gratification alone. All this we did while the soul starved itself to death.

Ours is the age of moral evasion. It is the age of Moral Energy Crisis. We have the tools. We have brain capacity. We pay unconscionable lip service to ideals, to bromides, clichés, platitudes, incantations, and hypocritical rhetoric about our souls, our spirit, about being connected to the earth. How can we even begin to talk about oneness with the environment, connecting with nature when we are so radically disconnected from who we are at the core, living lives unrelated to who we are, refusing to ultimately fulfil the final stages of our spiritual evolution and moral transformation? Like children deeply attached to their cribs, but who have no desire to live a life beyond it, we reject the conditions that would allow us to live lives beyond the spiritual crib—our own short-lived desires that extend only as far as the impending football game in three days.

God:

I have been thinking about the violence done to the soul in the name of tribalism. We do a great deal of talking about racism, and ethnocentrism, and nationalism. All these are variations on a pernicious aspect of our human condition: tribalism.

The biggest impediment to our spiritual advancement is tribalism. I believe that this is something You communicated to me earlier. You planted this seed of restlessness in me, this boredom with roots and with geographical kin. You placed this love of humanity in me and this deep desire to feel brotherhood for people regardless of their tribal affiliation. Today, our world is ravaged by tribal conflicts, ethnic purges and cleansing, and a tenacious desire for some to prove the superiority of their kind by an appeal to blood, ancestry, and national origin.

God, I implore You, more than any personal dream of my own, to make us all realize collectively before our world is destroyed, that any strike against another human being, regardless of his or her background of origin, is a strike against our holy collective humanity.

Make us realize that the stupid and artificial false markers of race (there is only one race, the human race) do nothing but carve our humanity into spheres that haven't any connection to reality. We hijack our moral lives according to a separatist tribal logic. We do such violence to our souls by slashing them into ethnic and racial pieces, fooling ourselves into thinking that these arbitrary categories name an essence we must embrace. No wonder we are a shallow people. What incentive is there to dig beneath the dividers we've all carved up if we can make cottage industries out of them and be rewarded well for such a foolish enterprise?

Oneness of humanity—which I feel committed to—has been the teaching of Jesus and of all the great religious sages. I have this dream, and in it I want to say to others: Think of our society now being attacked by a virulent pandemic, a catastrophic war or, less apocalyptic, a massive earthquake. They take the lives of your family, friends, and children, all those whom your meaningful life has been built around. All that you might have when you regain consciousness, recover from shock, or open your eyes after the trauma is the person next to you. You grope for the hand of that person under the debris and wreckage as you desperately search for signs of a life, close to you. The hand is that of a stranger, a radical Other: a black, a Jew, a Mexican, a heathen—any person outside the intimate sphere of your social milieu. Why wait to act from a default position? Why wait for a crisis to force you into brotherhood with the stranger. Life, proactive and pulsating is sitting, walking, and standing next to you. Right now, this moment. Take hold of it. The hand of the stranger that you would grope for so desperately is here. In the street. Meet him. Meet her. And recognize him as your brother. Recognize her as your sister. Right now. And be content. Nothing more. Nothing less.

We know that there are four principal blood types. They are dispersed among what is today described as the various human racial and ethnic groups. That is, there is no set of individuals who are regarded as belonging to a distinctive race who all exclusively share the same blood type. The four human blood types are allocated among all persons today regarded as black, white, Asian, and Indian—to name just a few of the tribal taxonomies under which individuals are classified.

Because we are united in one body through Christ, we are the legatees of a gift You have bequeathed to us. And it is anathema to the spirit of every variant of tribalism, whether it takes the form of cultural nationalism or racial particularity. This gift, Lord, is the humble capacity to genuflect before the other in a spirit of reciprocity, in respectful brotherhood and sisterhood, and say: "I am not so complete that I can resist handing over to you some part of my continued socialization and identity formation as a human being. With you, my friend, my humanity, regardless of its origins, continues to expand and will take me to places I could never have imagined."

I regard this gift-giving impulse as part of how we organically make Christ-like values as human beings. One says further in the genuflection: "We share a common humanity, and in the spaces of that sacred humanity something of the Divine is achieved. I open myself as a canvas on which you may inscribe your wisdom, teachings, and generosity—or whatever seeds of it you may have discovered in your own soul."

Tribal idolatry exists within, God. We spiritually tattoo our tribal identities by generationally passing them onto those in our clans. We psychologically clone our tribal imprints onto our kin while paying lip service to brotherhood. Our obsession with our tribal affiliations is a form of Obsessive Compulsive Disorder. Our tribal idolatry stems from deep narcissism that is born out of seeing oneself as a special type of person because of one's racial, ethnic, or national identity. We want to glorify and deify this "I." Each wants to live in a world where the other looks, acts, thinks and speaks like this "I," from which each derives his sense of worth simply because he lacks it in himself. We become interchangeable members in a pristine universe and when we look at each other we are in some way looking at ourselves. We can only reproduce this "I" en masse by tribal psychological cloning.

Today's fury over genetic cloning is one-sided—ethically perverse as it may be. We have been doing the same thing on the soul level for thousands of years. The moral perversion is that it has been sanctioned as a good thing. Tribal separatism rules our souls. And, God, if today I speak of brotherhood, what am I told? How am I greeted? Like a naïve child.

I want to march into the streets and shout in anger when a Gypsy is killed, when an Albanian, an Arab, a Jew, an African, a white southerner, an Asian, an Indian, a Haitian, a person because of her skin color, sexual orientation, religious belief, or a woman because she is a woman is tortured and maimed. I want to shout in rage my God, in the name of the collective damage that's done to our shared humanity.

I don't shout, though. I think of the lovers of humanity You have placed on this earth. Josephine Baker, for example, who sacrificed much of her life by adopting twelve children from all over the world, children from different nationalities, races, and religious backgrounds. One, a newborn infant of African parents was found in Paris in a trashcan on Christmas Eve. Two others, brother and sister, were found among the rubble in the aftermath of an Algerian war. Jews and Muslims, white orphans from Sweden and France, South American Indians, and even a Japanese child—all found their way into her loving care. Josephine, herself, God, a Black American woman who became the most celebrated black singer and dancer in 20th century France and all Europe, was lovingly adopted by Paris in 1926 when

America turned its back on her. She called her twelve children The Rainbow Tribe. She wanted to prove to the world that racism was taught, that her children could love each other despite their differences. And they did. I am inspired by her words: "Surely the day will come when color means nothing more than skin tone, when religion is seen uniquely as a way to speak one's soul; when birthplaces have the weight of a throw of the dice and all men are born free, when understanding breeds love and brotherhood."

Restore our belief in this shared humanity. Imprint upon our moral imagination the beauty of our restorative powers. We can restore our humanity. We have to look inside the souls you gave us and admit to the fear the explorer feels when he or she enters unchartered territory. Help us to sustain the faith in ourselves as we admit that we are encountering ourselves for the first time.

Emancipate us from the shame in admitting: "I do not know myself. And I never have. And I never will. Not if I continue living falsely by donning the non-universal tribal markers that prevent me from seeing the face of my own soul first, and thus cause me to hate and despise the faces and souls of others."

Carl Jung writes: "An epoch is like an individual. It has its own limitations."

In this millennium, deliver us, God, from the limitations of our epoch. Resurrect the spirit of the lonely moral giants who walk silently among us. Absolve us of our cortical oddities so that we may see them, and that we may welcome them.

Give our souls the appetitive and voracious hunger they ought to have. And let us not self-consume, Lord, the synthetic and ephemeral desires of our narcissistic egos to reproduce wretched etchings drawn from eyes that have never seen. Rather, I pray that we may have the foresight to take Your seedlings that sprout forth from each morning's dew and, one by one, plant them where we least expect them to grow: in that space called enmity that separates us from our adversaries when we stand before each other in rage and pride; in that space between faith and doubt that is the house of paralysis and mental confusion; in that space between reason and trauma where need becomes belief, but the mind imposes a deadly logic that obliterates the contemplative spirit in all of us, where the mind rejects the truth that the heart intuits; and in that space between activities of the practical business of life, and the stillness we feel when we are rendered senseless by beauty, by the incomprehensible, by the experiences for which no words can denote. May we call this space the House of Timelessness? Is it in that space that the spiritual revolution necessary to truly know You takes place? Is it the *agere contra*, the "positive resistance" that must take place in the dichotomous tensions within those spaces that we must choose in order to have knowledge of Your mysteries?

This is our birthright as co-participants with You in our destinies and life plans. You gave us this birthright, God. Help us to start the process of earning back the birthright we ignored. Help us, dear God, each step of the way.

My Dear Lord:

Are You tiring of my begging? Am I crazy for writing these letters? What is going to happen? I feel much closeness to You while I write—sometimes. And You know the rest of my story and what I am going to say. At other times, I feel like a fake. I feel that I am writing You these letters because I am responding to a voice that said: "Communicate to me through the talents I gave to you. Talk to me through your gifts." That's all, like a child obeying a parent without question, writing despite my better judgments. Was this Your voice? Or was it nothing more than a tired soul on the brink of death finding a way to pursue a spiritual realization in the form of a question? What is the talent I have given You? The gift to be an artist, to be a writer. And in what does the writing culminate? Not in books, not in journals, not in essays, not in anything tangible in this world.

But, right there, at the tip of all my fingers.

You've given me a blessed path. Still, there are moments when I believe I have lost You. The closeness dissipates. Then, I write out of the same stubbornness that refuses to give up a task once I have started it.

This could be a process of faith building. Even when I feel You are once again lost to me, something keeps my fingers typing in the hope that You will be found. Is that faith? At the height of my disbelief, my father wrote to me and said that it was through philosophy that I would be led right back to God. I laughed at the time because it was in my philosophical writings that I was waging my harshest battle against You.

Are You turning my battlefield into a truce camp? And what would the soldier do if his commander-in-chief took away his capacity to fight those whom he had considered his greatest adversaries?

No. Don't tell me right now. In the morning, perhaps. I'm reluctant to accept what I think the answer might be. I don't think I have the courage to withstand all that would be demanded of me.

Dear God:

Most of Your visions of our possibilities exist in what I would call *the not-yet-zone*. And the gift of Your dignity, the image of You in which we are made, is to bring those zones into existence. As Abraham Heschel states: "We live in a state of possible disclosures."

Open wide our moral imaginations and give us the explorative sense of adventure we need to unite those two spheres You've given us: the Eternal Divine and the Finite.

I had a very interesting conversation today. I was very distressed about certain forms of recklessness in our society. My friend, the philosopher Fred, said that he was surprised that people still believed in moral progress. The standard view among philosophers is that humankind advances in degrees. We regress, advance a bit, and then regress, but really, there is no progress. The drama of the human condition is our quest for moral advancement while our human constitution constantly pulls us down into the doldrums of depravity.

God, I don't believe that moral progress is not a sustainable condition. You know that even when I was an atheist, I was an even bigger hero worshipper than I am now. I had to be. Since I had exorcised You out of my life, I had to replace You. I replaced You with Man, Man the hero. Man, the benevolent and glorious god. I am still a hopeless romantic idealist. I suppose I shall always be. I will always believe in an ever-expansive range of human possibilities. But now I fervently believe, with all my heart (and sometimes the heart flounders God, You know that) that the heroism can only be sustained by a life lived close to You.

There are some who will say that in returning to You, I have robbed man of his proper estate, and that I have made the human into a lowly supplicant, a creaturely thing who stands obsequiously before an ineffable God whose consciousness cannot be grasped. I don't believe that. My belief that moral heroism requires You is testimony to Your strength rather than an indictment of human beings for their weakness. Since we are part of You and Your creation, and, since we did not make ourselves in the metaphysical sense of creation, then our deepest and most enduring sense of efficacy, of strength and moral robustness must stem from You.

When we join You, we become an invincible team. You remember that this was one of the attractions of getting back to You. There was this realization that hit me: instead of fighting Him why don't I just join forces with Him. Together we could make an incredible team.

Now that I have made the decision to join You, I can't say that I feel cozy companionship. You know that in trying to build the life of faith the difficulties I encounter often leave me depressed, emotionally exhausted, and with a sense of hopelessness.

I must work harder. Order and precision have ruled my intellect; reason has been its guiding principle. Chaos and turbulence have brewed and festered like a mush of rot in my soul for years.

I know that the quick fixes I wish for when it comes to developing my relationship with You are unrealistic. Besides, have I not asked You to spare me the shortcuts? As a philosopher and a teacher of ethics, I know that there are no shortcuts.

Spiritual Boot Camp is a noble and enterprising struggle. Again, my good Lord, I only ask that You not let go of my hand. Hold it tightly. That will give me courage not to abandon the road that I have chosen.

The road that You have chosen.

The road that we have chosen.

And if I promise to squeeze your hand, will You keep holding on to mine? Will You?

Do You promise?

God:

I'm excited about seeing Grandma tomorrow. I'm frightened every time I see her because I think it'll be the last time. Why make her death so protracted? I often thought my spiritual emancipation would come after she died. I thought she would appear to me in dreams, or something like that, and that my longing for her goodness, her beauty and spiritual cleanliness would bring a profound change in me. Are You keeping her alive so that I can tell her that some of her most persistent prayers might yet be answered? That I am trying to find my way back to You? Are You? But I have this sinking feeling in my stomach that if I tell her, You will release her. And when she goes, she will have taken away a part of this earth from me. A light will have gone out of the world for all of us who know and love her.

I think I'll tell her about these letters I'm writing to You. I have told no one about them and I don't plan on ever telling anyone. But I believe the letters would make her happy. She won't be able to talk to me, but still, with difficulty, she will manage a smile.

I know she still loves You. She hangs on to life out of the love You have given her, her love for the world and for her children. So, I'll tell her and watch the twinkle in her eyes and know that her heart is smiling. I want to give her a final sense of victory. I want to let her know the power of her incredible prayers. She needs to know that that boy she prayed for, who vowed that it was immoral to believe in God, has now, without being able to fully articulate the reasons, vowed to give his life to God in the way God chooses to use it.

She needs to know that You continue to affirm her prayers despite no longer being able to pray out loud in her inimitable way. She needs to know that just because her capacity for speech is gone that it does not mean that she has been rendered inaudible in your universe. I need to tell her: "Grandmother, you speak to Him with your incredible voice, and your will to live, and He hears you. He listens, and He has granted you something that I know you desperately wanted for years: He called me back into His Holy Embrace. And, lonely, dejected, unhappy, and tormented I ran, and ran. I'm still running because those arms keep opening wider and wider and wider. God bless you, Granny."

God:

I'm nervous about my students. I am unhappy with them. What am I doing teaching students in the middle of the boonies amidst barren cornfields? Sometimes I despise them immensely. Sometimes, I feel great love for them, and my strong paternal urges overtake my better judgments and I pamper them too much. Help me to understand their despair and their animosity toward life and, occasionally, toward me. I have given them everything I possibly can. I have tried to nurture them and raise them to the highest standards I believe they can aspire to. Why do I feel hostility from them? Is it because I am a foreigner? Is it because they are not used to a person of color instructing them? How can I prevent myself from projecting my deepest fears onto them? How can I admit to anyone but you that I am afraid of them?

Give me the maturity to rise above my fears and the wisdom to see their inadequacies as something to work with instead of wishing them out of existence. I keep thinking: "My God, but these are college students. They should know better."

Perhaps the disappointment is too great, and I have staked too much of my happiness on my capacity to be a perfect teacher.

Make things right for me. There I've said it. Please make things right for me in this situation. That's all I can ask for right now.

Thanks for a lovely weekend with my family. Thank You for the opportunity to see my grandmother once more. Dear God, I feel overwhelmingly helpless when I am there. To witness her absolute helplessness and dependence on the goodness of others is a reminder of our frailty and creatureliness as human beings. It is a reminder that we can go from being self-sufficient one day, with the capacity to laugh and talk, cook and eat and take care of our daily toiletries, to being rendered mute, paralyzed, and unable to function the next day. Feeding is via a tube inserted through her stomach. As I helped my mother clean her up and as I watched her replenish her feeder, I pondered the meaning of care, of dependency, and of human dignity. I meditated on ways in which the latter is inextricably bound up with the love and goodness of other people who extend their time, energies, and compassion to those in need—and in a non-condescending and non-patronizing manner.

Grandmother is lucky that she is in a position to be so deeply loved, that her very discomfort is often anticipated before she experiences it, that her hands are held frequently, her temples massaged, and her face littered with kisses. But what of those who have no one, rotting away more from loneliness than from filth in nursing homes? What will become of them? What of those who sacrificed their lives to the upkeep of others? What of those who care for those who betrayed them? What of them? What have they done to deserve that? And, of course, I wonder what will become of me. I have no children and perhaps will never have children for reasons You know all too well. So, who will take care of me? Who will feed or clean me when I am no longer able to take care of the minimum of my body's needs?

I feel sad for my mother. So much of her life is dedicated to taking care of her own mother. What will happen to her after her mother dies? "Where will I end up after I've been deprived of my purpose in life?" my mother wept one afternoon.

I ask dear God, that You grant her a sense of her own uniqueness in her multifaceted nature. Relieve her of the fixation on a self-image that will no longer serve her when the others on whom she needs to reinforce that image are no longer there. Anchor her to a sense of survival that is outside her role as only a caregiver.

God:

The philosopher Jean-Paul Sartre says: "True radicalism lies in the intentions we have rather than in the goals that we carve for ourselves." I have been wondering about this. So, help me out on this issue. We can give the appearance of sharing similar goals. After a while, however, they appear foreign because the intentions behind them are radically different.

So, intention is the key. But I wonder: What does it mean today to have a radical intention? It seems as if our minds, our dreams, and our intentions are re-programmed for us. We are overdetermined creatures in the sense that we are made to know early in life that certain intentions are rewarded and penalized, not according to their moral status, but their usefulness and social popularity and utility.

I have no desire to have radical intentions. I have tried to live close to my heart and to follow the natural rhythms that write themselves there. I've said this before. Deep truths about the Self need to be re-stated. I believe that the pressures of modern life have the power to make me deaf to the immutable truths that are a part of me.

But what would it mean to have a radical intention? Is my intention to seek You radical? Is it radical within the context of who I am, what I was, what I struggle vainly against? Is it radical to will myself to want to simply become a man of God, to be spiritually pure while I remain, sometimes, agnostic?

The thing that haunts me, God, is that I cannot understand how my fingers are typing these words when right now, this very minute, I don't feel close to You. I struggle with the issue of intimacy with You and yet, I summon the will to continue seeking You. Could it be that once a creature of habit has made the commitment to find You, that he becomes incapable of not fulfilling his commitment regardless of his feelings at any given moment?

No. This is not true of someone who just identified himself as one who lives close to the heart. I live close to my heart, yet I don't have intimacy with myself. I cannot have this intimacy because I embrace and honor only select parts of who I am; more particularly, I love the future self, *the not-yet-self;* the self I wish to become. I am, therefore, like a breathing abstraction, stranger to myself yet close to a crucial part of myself—the self I am remaking. Is this then what it means to have a radical intention? Are my intentions so absurd that a detached observer could reasonably say: "Son, you live your life as if miracles were the norm?"

One could ask how a recovering atheist could expect to accomplish everything I hope to accomplish. Old fashioned common sense informs me that one does not travel all this psycho-spiritual distance away from one's creator and then decide after a long time that the journey is lonely, that he wants to get back to the safety and metaphysical security of he who made him and expect that all that has been lost should be recovered so quickly. Some may say it can be done, that all one has to do is give one's life over to You, mouth some platitude about You being a savior and that's that.

God, You know my intentions. You know that my intention is not to get to that state where I can find myself writhing on some church ground screaming Your name with tears flowing. My intentions are neither as dramatic, nor as cosmetic. What I want is to be so close to You that I walk in a state of equanimity even when I am anxious—paradoxical as that may sound—because Your presence is vividly felt, like the sensation of some magnetic current that buoys me lightly from the ground. My intention is to have You lodged so firmly in my heart, that I need never utter Your name again, plead with You again, or be conscious that You are separate from me.

God, I don't believe my overall intention is radical. It is simple. Either that, or my present spiritual ignorance keeps me from knowing the category in which to place it, but here it is: *I want to be like You.*

Father:

I keep wondering about the state of tension involved in having wisdom in one sphere of life, and the lack of will that prevents me from exercising it in others. Here's the deal: As a writer I know that I discover myself in the act of writing. It's an old cliché that rings true. All writers know that regardless of outlines and plot structures, once they begin writing, characters write themselves into existence and take control. Unplanned events occur that were not part of the consciously constructed outline of the writer.

Specialists say that surrendering to the writing process allows the unconscious to express itself. Still, there is a sense of living within the realm of the unknown when one lives deeply and inwardly as a writer. That is, one trusts that in the process of actual writing, a type of life—existence if you will—emerges that has its own logic, order, and indescribable magic that cannot be anticipated prior to the act of writing.

I know this. I have lived it repeatedly. So, what is the problem with taking that approach and applying it to life? Why can't I trust Your capacity to saturate my life fully enough to allow myself, for just one moment, to live within the realm of the unknown?

Oh, it really is tiring to always live by the militant and steely force of will. I long to delve into the realm of the unknown and feel comfort in that form of existence, knowing that Your intervention in my life eclipses the natural felicity I think I have for knowing how my will ought to be functioning at each hour of the day.

How I long for the capacity to pray for something that I desperately want and need, something without which my life wouldn't be meaningless, but disappointing. And yet, in praying and not receiving what I want I would be filled with serenity and acceptance, *knowing* that You have granted, in Your denial, a blessing that I cannot see in my corporeally finite and spiritually infantile state. To believe that You ultimately grant us not always what we ask for, but what is always in our best interest as beings made in Your likeness. My grandmother used to try to get us all to live that type of life. But always there was my will and the maniacal desire to shape my universe according to the power of my will.

But if fixation on the will and its desires are illusions, then I have been living partly by illusions. But can that be a bad thing, Lord? Are most of us strong enough to live without the comforting veils of illusions? The will is what You gave us, and it is what allows us to be co-participants in the creation and then realization of our destiny.

My addiction in life has been to the power of my will. I have then been addicted to an illusion. But how could I have called myself a philosopher otherwise? How could I have dedicated my life to a profession which alleges to have as its goal the acquisition of truth and the penetration of the reality behind illusions?

I want to be able to quietly accept that this affair with the will stems from a deep fear of the world. I want to finally admit God, that for all my intellectual bravado, determination, and discipline, that deep down inside I have always been afraid of being beaten up by the schoolyard bullies. The greater the fear I felt, the more I hardened my will, and the more I worshiped it. My will. Always Intransigent. Implacable. Defiant.

Why admit this if you know me better than anyone else? I need some tangible evidence of my visibility. And it is not often that I feel this visibility in the world. That's sad since I believe that it is in our struggles with each other as human beings that we realize our humanity, and that we come close to granting any truth to that biblical adage: God made man in his own image. The image of man today is not always an inspiring sight, but it cannot be your fault. Again, it comes back to the illusions to which we are attached. I fail to realize this and so do most of my fellow brothers and sisters on earth. The illusions are not meant to be permanent attachments—they are part of the enlightenment tools we temporarily need to build and achieve our humanity, and then our soul maturity.

I believe that if I can start by working on my own crippled humanity then I won't be so crushed when others fail in theirs. If I admit that I am a sometimes-helpless dependent creature—dependent on the goodness of others—then I can begin to understand the source of my harshness when others fail me. I have placed an unfair burden and responsibility on them. The message I have sent them is:

You are to be the Hercules of my world. My precarious and brittle hold on life needs to be bolstered by your consistent bravery and goodness. If You can't be these things, then I cease to believe in the goodness of the world, and my sense of purpose will disappear.

Is it any wonder that much of my life has been spent in anger, disappointment, and loneliness? Is it any wonder that the happiness I have experienced has all too often been predicated on the future: the future heroic moral selves that will come into existence and be my playmates and make the world feel safe for me?

Sometimes I am like a frightened child who feels like a cripple in a world he struggles to understand but feels helpless to fully comprehend. And so, I cover up this helplessness and infuse my soul, my intellect, and emotions with a thick coating of confidence. But now there are small cracks, everywhere. Behind the peeling, fading, cracking veneer stands a naked child. The symptoms of my sickness catch up with me. My body aches. My head aches. My chest explodes in revolt. I beat the tirades of the body into submission by pushing my body on, and on with maniacal endless energy. My body has never lied to me. Its symptoms have always indicated a deeper malaise that I treat with a dose of sternness and more will—will imposed over will, over more will. Will layering will, smothering a deeper neurosis.

I am exhausted. Can you feel it? From as far back as seven there has been a constant throbbing pain in my head which has never left me. It wavers in degrees, but the heavy sensation has never ever left. It is not physiological. It is not biological. It is a deep spiritual malaise. What are my deepest fears, God? Reveal them to me and help me to stomach them. Will I love myself after the revelations? To be an archeologist of the soul is to risk exposure, the consequences of which one might not be equipped to stomach. Have I ever truly loved myself? I am caught between the Scylla of mundane Self, and the Charybdis of Ideal Self—the self I wish to become. Self-contentment and satisfaction are not psychic states I can feel comfortable with. How can I? What incentive would exist for me to grow? What incentive would there be for me to aspire to something which I can truly be proud of?

If I think about it, Lord, it seems to me that unconditional love is something that I have not fully experienced. What is it to really love someone unconditionally and even more than that—what does it mean to love oneself unconditionally? If I love myself without conditions, then what motivates me to become a better person? If You love me unconditionally what incentive is there for me to emerge from whatever it is that is rotten and complacent in me? Rottenness. Don't we all have a bit of that in us? When others love us unconditionally, how do we move beyond moral laziness? But part of me does want to be loved for everything I am now, and it is because of fear. I am afraid that there are parts of me that cannot be changed, or parts that would require vast amounts of time for change to emerge.

Could I live without love for that long of a period of time? Could I live without self-love and still survive? If I don't have unconditional self-love and unconditional love from others, then what will enable me to endure life when life is tough, and when affirmations from the world are not forthcoming? But if I do have the unconditional love I desire, will I have the will and the discipline to recognize spiritual regression and immaturity when I am afflicted with them? Will I even have the desire to halt them, knowing that no matter how low I fall I will have love?

You see my dilemma? Is there a solution? This is, among other things, what has dogged me. This is what makes the relationship to myself stormy. Not surprisingly, this makes my dealings with others charged and sometimes a little too intense. I burn others out with that intensity, and then I catch fire in the process.

And so, once more, I ask that You empower me with a will to fight this dilemma. Strange, isn't it? In one breath I am talking about the problems of the will and the illusions they spawn. In another breath I am imploring You to strengthen my will to face the challenges of that dilemma bravely. Perhaps the will is inescapable, and I should be praying for the desire to have a certain type of relationship to it. What is that ideal relationship? Is that the key? I want to say: no shortcuts, God. Although it is tempting to pray for them, I have the feeling that I am ultimately praying for things that will make my life more difficult. To pray for shortcuts would be to simplify my life.

Why this love affair with struggle? Am I a masochist at heart?

I have the feeling that no worthwhile journey should be an easy one. An easy journey would rob me of the challenge of what it means to be a human being in the exalted sense of the term. The path of least resistance would deprive me of the potential You endowed me with. But again, Lord, I am worried. Am I strong enough to live with all that I am praying for, knowing full well that the ways in which You answer prayers might not match the spirit in which they are uttered? This is the big question: *I can pray the prayers. Can I live the answers?*

Still, I am motivated to keep asking You to give me the strength to live those answers. It is another route to faith-building. Faith does not strike with one blow. Faith does not seem to be something that I can suddenly have and have for keeps. I catch glimpses of what it is. I feel it in one short precious moment, and then— it's gone!

Gone for months.

And I spend the rest of my time looking for it again. I try to recapture my emotional state by asking myself: What were my thoughts, my fantasies, and my mood just before I had them?

But, perhaps, in the very act of living, living despite my inability to feel faith deeply, living and hoping, hoping timidly that I will have it the next day, perhaps *that* is faith. Maybe faith really isn't this mystical phenomenon I thought it was. It is something rather mundane such as: planning for the future when we do not even know if the next hour of life is guaranteed; getting on that plane without knowing for sure if it will land safely; spending ten years in school and completing a Ph.D. without ever knowing if the world I so desperately wanted to purchase with that credential would be mine; seeking love in those moments when one is convinced one cannot find it; or, a family deciding to give birth to a child despite pre-natal testing that reveals that is has myriad congenital birth defects. Perhaps, Lord, all these are instantiations of faith. Its prerequisite is hope, which You instilled in us. Perhaps we are all walking creatures of faith without knowing it, each of us em-bodiments of something ideal and wonderful and, yet we spend a lifetime seeking it in the lives of others.

Wanting a sign from You, not knowing if I will receive it but acting as if I will. Is that faith? If it is, then I ought to take respite in it and acknowledge the honor and dignity it has brought to my life. I am filled with what I already am, Lord. Let me take this knowledge, run with it and honor it by seeing how already full I am of something I have spent my life craving. Grant me and grant my brothers and sisters in the world with the strength of character to guide our lives and, especially, our darkest moments by this newly discovered faith.

God:

Can You explain my nightmares and visions of an apocalypse that I have had even during the years I was a principled atheist? In those dreams none of the light switches work. I keep trying to turn them on and they won't come on. The world is in complete darkness, and I am terrified. Sometimes, I'm trying to find my family. I accept, eerily so, in the dreams, that darkness is the natural state of the world. I accept that all the lights are out and that they are going to be out for a long time.

It could be that the darkness I am encased in is a state of being that I personally have traveled and will have to travel before coming into any light. But in this culture, darkness is *verboten*. It's all feel-good spiritual massaging and immediate light once you can pay for it at the nearest bookstore, or to any advertised fortune teller wheeler-dealer-reader.

Children are afraid of the dark for good reasons. Their motor skills have not been adequately honed for them to navigate their way in the dark. They have not experienced themselves enough in the world. This lack of experience and lack of intimate contact with the world in its varied dimensions place them in an existential predicament: The darkness suffocates the dim memory of the lighted world they have contact with. The darkness has the power to communicate with them: *This is all there is.* It announces itself as permanent. They cry out in the dark for a hand to turn on the lights because they have absorbed too little of the temporary lights of the world to be convinced that the darkness that envelops them is not temporary. It can be overcome by switching on the lights within their own souls.

Who is that provides the first impetus to turn on the inward lights of our souls? Our parents? Our spiritual teachers? And what of those who have not had sufficient contact with such soul-igniters, where can they find the guidance to turn on their own lights? Yes, Lord, I know we are born with light, but it is here on earth that we work out our humanity and our Divine natures. And it is through others that we learn those skills. Those others are Your appointees.

And so, God, I return to my initial concern. Can we fault each other for remaining at the stage of spiritual infancy when our spiritual guides and leaders hide from us the dark rooms we have to pass through before we can get to light? Again, we manufacture multiple illusions that give off fake light. Is it any wonder that after maturing into adulthood we remain just as afraid of the darkness as children are? We are still afraid of being swallowed by it.

God:

I'm still thinking about my last letter to You about the fear of the darkness, and the way we are culturally disinclined to accept any spiritual message that comes tainted with even a patina of darkness.

It is all predicated on fear. We induce willed deafness because we fear. We fear that if we acknowledge the darkness, we might not have the conviction in knowing that all life is a value whose expression is found in the audacity to go on deeply living—living BIG. Even those of us who pay lip service to being open to truth, open to the wisdom of the great seers of the ages, know that we tacitly and, often unwittingly, lay specific conditions on the terms by which we receive truth.

We are often not receptive to truth. Partial truths, perhaps, or truths colored and rusted in such a way that a great deal of interpretive maneuverings would have to take place to wrest anything authentic from them. How splendid it would be to be free to receive truth in any way that it chose to reveal itself to us. How heroic would be the sight of one who loved truth so much—as opposed to selected truths that add nutritive value to one's material and worldly life—that she could trust in its ability to fruitfully enhance life in ways that, in her spiritual infancy, she could not fully comprehend.

God:

I'm wondering what the great voices of the on-going 21st Century will sound like? What in us will they appeal to? Will we hear them when what is deepest in us remains hidden? Voices that reprimand and reproach are tolerated only so long as they make us feel good about ourselves in the end. I'm as good as any other person, so anyone who speaks to me needs to make sure that I'm evaluated and then judged equally.

But am I equal to all? We are not all equals, are we? There are some people who are better than me. They are spiritually and morally superior to me, and it's good that I can admit this, is it not? I can pin my aspirational identity on a model of moral perfection.

Why do people resent the idea that there are people who are better than they are? Is it fear, or arrogance? It is, I believe, false pride and deep-seated resentment at the realization that to be as spiritually good as the other person, one has to work very hard, delay much gratification, and stomach a great deal of disquieting truths about oneself that overturns one's deepest self-image.

Moral health requires a spiritualized diet that is often sparse, ascetic, and unglamorous. But our collective metabolic rate exceeds the minimum capacity for reflective and measured digestion of the teachings we desperately crave. Uttering unconscionable lip service to new age chants, incantations, platitudes, truisms, and intonations of varying registers, we gorge ourselves without realizing that we are starving because all the accoutrements we take as food do not hit the mark. We still emerge hungry for something more—something deeper. That which is in need of spiritual nourishment is the enduring.

Lord:

Happy and patiently I am sitting here, waiting for You to write Your intentions into my life. I wish to be Your servant and carry out the edicts that You will program into my soul. Simply put: I'm tired of being lost and lonely. And now, like the rising phoenix, I dream of casting aside the debris and detritus that have intermittently entombed my soul. I yearn to take my place among the pantheon of moral perfectionists that You have anointed.

Lift up my heart, God. Emblazon my soul with a new hunger that returns me time and time again to You for its countenance and replenishment. Let the greatest of my desires and the weakest form of my fading strength commingle to find sweet repose in You, the Host.

Psalm 40 inspires me:

I waited, waited for the Lord;
Who bent down and heard my cry,
Drew me out of the pit of destruction,
Out of the mud of the swamp
Set my feet upon rock,
Steadied my steps,
And put a new song in my mouth,
A hymn to our God.
Many shall look on in awe
And they shall trust in the Lord.

More on the subject of love, God. The novelist Jeanette Winterson writes that art leaves nobody out, but that it cannot condescend. We have to climb up if we want the extraordinary view. That's a rather beautiful metaphor for how love ought to function. Why should love condescend to the lowest common denominator in any of us? By what sort of impertinence dare any of us think that we have a right to love by virtue of our lowest feature. Should we not climb to get the extraordinary view on life that love offers? What becomes of love when it condescends? Doesn't it become too mired in the elusive and shallow present? Doesn't it lose its inherent quality and become indistinguishable from any other fleeting emotion?

People who want to be loved for their vices and flaws haunt me. I am haunted because I battle with the same desire. I am haunted because the desire to be morally coherent, which is the antithesis of the desire to be loved for one's flaws, is tiring. It is often tedious.

It bores me.

I don't, however, want my love to be in danger of becoming just another manufactured feeling that qualifies itself according to whims that come in and out of fashion, be they the whims of others, of our culture, the world, or even my own whims that try to whore their way into intimacy with the deeper part of my soul.

Can the best within my soul be robbed by the cheapness of thoughtless desires that seek to underestimate the irreplaceable value of the soul that You gave me? I think it could. I have fought against the cheap element, Lord, so hard that sometimes I think that the battle and the discipline to maintain it have cost me part of my humanity. It is only now, as I am forced to fight for my spiritual maturity and evolution, that I wish to engage in the process of humanizing myself once more.

Lord:

Like a lot of people, I fear death. Why this obsessive fear of death? I know that it partly has to do with not accepting fully the idea of an everlasting life. Immortality still eludes me. But I can't rush the belief, and rushing can never be a good remedy for anything, even agony itself. I am recommencing my relationship with You after a long hiatus. I am struggling to find You again, seeking the old lover whom I tossed aside in anger, hubris, and spite. In time, I will develop my own emotional relationship to the notion of an everlasting life with You. If I told You, God, that Heaven seems like an abstraction would you feel jilted? I must be honest. At this stage of my spiritual progression, the concept of Heaven eludes me. It's not that I think there is no such dimension, only my mind cannot reach it.

Help me.

For the sake of my dying grandmother, I need to have some idea of it. When I watch the deterioration of her mangled body I wonder: Why does she have to suffer so much? What has she done?

This is her purgatory. I believe this. And so, when she dies, she is going straight to angels who must comb her beautiful black hair and prepare her for Your loving embrace. I must believe this. It is her life and its beauty that is my emotional impetus for coming to terms, not just with death, but with the concept of an afterlife. Perhaps a great many others and I are driven by conscience and emotional longing to believe in an afterlife. There is a sense in which I think that the sacrifices my grandmother has made, and the protracted death she is experiencing, are interpretable within a much larger framework than the one I have at my disposal.

Our moral imagination is stretched by the traumas of our inability to comprehend much that we experience.

It also seems to me that what I need to come to terms with, or more loosely speaking, what I might experiment with, and I ask your guidance again in this area, is to contemplate the notion that we were all created for some end. We cannot truly know the end though, given the rise in the increase in psychic assistance that so many people are craving. Many think that they know these ends—and perhaps they do. But if I accept the idea that I was created for some end and come to terms with the supremacy of Your end for my life, then my anguish over death ought to dissipate gradually.

This is not a matter of solving a riddle. It means comprehending, as a gifted discerner, that Your end is the best thing for my life. It is realizing that I have a limited perspective, a small view of my total life (including my afterlife). Any judgments that I make about this end will be ineffective because the purview of my range of vision and insight are limited.

But the real challenge is expanding this limited view. It simply can't be a matter of will, can it? Is there some simple disciplinary strategy that I can adopt in the name of an expanded consciousness? Can I force myself to have certain experiences with a view to extracting some insight that I piece together in the form of manufactured wisdom? Wisdom needs time before it becomes habituated into practice.

But, Lord, I also find the issue of wisdom perplexing. Wisdom seems to be bestowed on others through grace. People speak of having unreflective understanding that was not the result of disciplined thinking, or relaxed meditation. Instead, it seemed to have burrowed its way into their minds all very naturally. So, my question is this: If this is Divine Grace how can I get it? Does anyone have a right to it?

This realization then, that one is in possession of some special wisdom, is a gift. The recurring theme of the gift returns in my letters to You. It's as if You provide the outlet as a way for me to work out the themes without the pedantic and forced quality that accompany such writing in its academic format.

If the deepest form of wisdom then, is a gift, we are going to be in big trouble thinking and hoping for such gifts as our right. So, the challenge is to go through life without thinking one deserves the gift, and to believe it. It would be easy to refrain from expecting the gift for self-righteous and egotistical reasons. Such a stance would make me feel better about myself.

What I want is to create a way of life that is satisfying in itself so that at the end of it all, even if I had never received the gift, I would still be able to find pleasure in acts of living that are rewarding in themselves. But in this seductive age, I want to be able to regard my life and the acts I create as paths to good living as valuable because they are intrinsically good, not because of the rewards society gives to them. How many original human beings sacrifice their dreams because they lack the strength to stand and bask in the glory of goodness for its own sake? That appreciation of goodness is absent because it would have to be traced back to something intrinsically good in the individual. But how to achieve this in our characters when we are inundated by modes of appraisal via market fads, monetary potential, and fleeting societal norms?

Is this conception of goodness merely underrated, or is it viewed as an eccentricity? In an age when originality is constantly decried as a myth, we are at a loss to differentiate poseurs from authentic persons. Now we go to great lengths to prove to others that we are original. Nothing can shock us anymore, therefore, how will we differentiate ourselves? However hard we try, very few are convinced.

I have a feeling that the capacity to live silently is going to be one way in which we can capture our humanity in the midst of the noise pollution we face every day. It is the noise of ceaseless activity.

It is, above all, God, the noise I carry within myself.

But You know that I don't equate silence with indifference, or worse, with the feeling that one can't make a difference so one had better not risk anything by saying not anything. What is this new silence that I am feeling, God?

Silence is a method of distancing ourselves and of disowning a language that has taught us primarily to look outward at the world, and self-centeredly inward. It is this capacity to uncover our buried humanity and buried moral language in our souls that I wish to discover. I want to be silent while still speaking with my fellow human beings. This silence means that while speaking I refrain from being beguiled by the seductive language of ongoing human socialization. There must be a part of my soul that remains private, and it is in this private domain that the new silence must take place. This, Lord, will be our secret meeting place. I think of it as a new consummation. My soul is clogged and that, God, is why I am restlessly unfulfilled, empty, and insatiable despite achievements. My soul is clogged with everything but the seeds of Your truths that I have repudiated.

And what will this new silence bring? I have felt this new disposition developing, and it is part of the reason for my return to You, God. It haunts me. It burns me. It lies at the base of my artistic pursuits. What I feel churning away inside of me, and what I want for my fellow humans is *healthy moral shame*; moral shame not at what we are, but at our failure to realize our inherent potential to become what we were created to be. Give us, dear Lord, *the gift of moral becoming.*

Here, in the midst of this confusion about growth in silence—which I simply cannot find because the noise I carry within is combustible and I burn, I burn, I burn—I take emotional repose in the words of one of your Trappist monks, Thomas Merton. I recorded his words at the height of my atheism. And now, life itself speaks for itself. Merton writes in *The Seeds of Contemplation*: "The truest solitude is not something outside you, not an absence of men or of sound around you; it is an abyss opening up in the center of your own soul. And this abyss of interior solitude is created by a hunger that will never be satisfied with any created things."

And in *The Monastic Journey* he asserts: "The contemplative life has nothing to tell you except to reassure you and say that if you dare to penetrate your own silence and dare to advance without fear into the solitude of your own heart, you will truly recover the light and capacity to understand what is beyond words and beyond explanations because it is too close to be explained."

In living alone this past year, God, here is what I do know for sure: I have some psychological insight, but little self-intimacy. The ruthlessness and self-discipline that I apply to my life are forms of self-hatred. I compulsively pound the treadmill, I jog seven miles each day in the park, and I cannot see the flowers and the blue sky. I cannot stop to listen to the birds sing joyously as I share a habitat with them. Some invisible force hauls me though air. It spawns a make-believe soldier foolishly trapped in some escapist crusade, some self-transcending drama that is limited by my very creatureliness. I resent my finitude. And so, my body seems bent on eluding the joy it's capable of experiencing. And yet, that's not completely true. I feel this capacity for joy. I dance alone and sing constantly to myself, and often when I am with others I truly experience the joys of the world in ways that leave me happy as a child. But are such experiences and the accompanying states of mind constitutive of who I am, or are they merely character understudies that I draw upon from time to time?

And what is the antidote? How can I live fully in the world without thinking that balance is for emotional cripples? I wonder what I fear in allowing myself to see the world as a benevolent gift from You, rather than a quasi-battlefield I must both run from and fight with?

In time I feel that You will reveal to me the fears that clog my soul and prevent me from claiming what my intellect and my convictions suggest: That the world at large is my home, that my humanity is my unfailing companion; and that my character, rather than something to be transcended, is the raw material from which to construct a new relationship with You, and a new way towards becoming a new being.

Let the heart honor what the mind suggests is right. Let fear and distrust dissipate, and instead, forge a calm hand with a temperate intellect.

Dear God:

I find it maddening that on the very day I complain to You about being abandoned by my father I should receive a letter from him.

Is he mad? He remains convinced of his inebriated visions: that he will receive the Nobel Prize for Peace; a great Holocaust will destroy Jamaica; and that he will emerge as the country's seraphic leader of the revolution in the name of Jesus Christ his eternal Commander-in-Chief.

He is supremely assured that You have guaranteed him "two hundred percent" that he will be internationally celebrated as the greatest musician to have ever lived. This last declaration comes against the backdrop of his non-involvement with music for over several decades.

He is confident that a great plague will wipe out his country, and that the innocent and the wicked alike ought to perish. He speaks of fallen angels and demons with teeth as sharp as knives attacking him at night. He wails for the sons he abandoned, the family he repudiated, yet is convinced of the rectitude of his decision to sacrifice everything for You. He said he was called out to do battle as one of Your soldiers.

Here he is, a man cut off from civilization, a hermit who is planning musical scores for musicians long dead. He refuses to accept their deaths. He thinks that they will find him in the mountains and together they will perform in a musical revolution that will change the world.

He says he cannot call my name without weeping. He refers to me as his precious first born.

Do You think that he is a schizophrenic, God? I think he might well be. And then, I am haunted by how much his prognostications have stood the test of time. Without knowing anything of my life he has predicted much of what has taken place. And always, he claims to be acting under your auspices. I remember once, Lord, right after I got my baccalaureate when he ordered me in one of his fiery letters to write my doctoral thesis on Thomas Merton. I tossed his letter aside.

Who was Thomas Merton? Whoever he was, no self-respecting philosopher would write a thesis on his work. He was not a philosopher.

Well, isn't it strange how Thomas Merton's great works have played such an incredible role in my spiritual development? How have his books found their way into my life as gifts from friends who don't even believe in You?

God, there are so many predictions my father made about my life. At the height of my atheism, I remember him telling me once that all my atheistic writings were part of my "confessions," and that I should not worry about them. He said I would come back to You as a child weeping softly. When I asked how he could be certain of such things he said he and I were cut from the same cloth and that You had told him everything about my life.

What to do about him, Lord? What to do? All my life I fought against this man whom I have loved deeply. The tears of agony, the waiting, the longing for the solace of his arms and the kisses of his lips against my brow turned to bitterness. He was called out to do service in Your army. You were the drafter who stole the sole treasure of my childhood and replaced it with an insatiable appetite for something I could never retrieve: the love of my dear, sweet Papa. How I longed to gaze into those piercing green eyes that made me think of the sun. How I longed for those eyes that saw right through me and made me feel: *He is like the sun. If I get too close to him, I will burn, but I'm better off burning in his inebriated visions than living in loneliness.*

Yes, Lord, that is what I felt. And then, he was gone.

And You have been my greatest competitor.

So, what happens now?

Where am I going to?

How are your restorative powers working, Lord? Tell me. Whisper them to me. Show me a loving sign. Wrap your arms around me, God. I cannot fight You anymore. It is to You I wish to surrender, to yield in humble submission. Hold me and let me weep deeply into Your heart.

Hold me, for just one fleeting moment.

God:

I feel homeless and rootless. I know that sounds ironic given my celebration of rootlessness as a means to maturity. I have taken for granted the idea that a life of wandering complements the ways of one who seeks self-transformation. Since for a long time my desire has been to inflict an honorable death to the old self, I really shouldn't be complaining.

But rootlessness is weighing me down. If I am to prosper spiritually and grow into a transformed self, to have a soul-change, if you will, then I ought to be willing to live out this restlessness and desist in seeking quick solutions. I think once more of the spiritual malaise. I must let the disease run its course.

Disease. Dis-ease. Sickness. These features of contemporary life first struck me as an immigrant in America. In the Caribbean we rarely went to doctors for common ailments. One allowed the body to recover naturally from certain sicknesses. The readiness to remedy all minor ailments has not only subverted the natural healing capacities of the body but it has made us oblivious to the connections between physical ailments and spiritual deprivations. Again, to acknowledge this connection would mean slowing down our frenetic pace in the world. To slow down would be to disrupt what we take to be the natural rhythm of a successful activity-achievement-oriented life.

God, give me strength to discern this malaise and to acquire the skills of good interpretation. Teach me to feel, feed, hear and listen to the sickness to learn the ways out of sickness and the path to organic health. Give me the courage to hear my wounds as they cry. And grant me the strength to resist the temptation to cover my ears and assuage my wounds with false prescriptions.

God:

I am awed by Your communication through mediums strange and complex, yet, simple and unobtrusive. I am surprised by the messengers You send into my life. Even when I was an atheist, time after time, You sent your emissaries to speak with me. There were moments when I felt the rancor rising in me and I wanted to tell them that the only thing I needed to be saved from was parasitic, mindless brain-dead quacks such as themselves. But always, or at least, in most cases, something restrained me. Perhaps it was the face of my grandmother; perhaps it was the way that she, not by way of words, but through simple kindness, radiated the best example of how a truly God-giving person should behave. In remembering how she exemplified Your ideals, I now thank You for filling me with the equanimity of spirit that has allowed me to listen patiently to Your messengers as they tried to impart lessons I was not ready to learn.

I am still not always ready. For example, what were You trying to tell me that time when I flew into Ithaca? I had asked You for some small sign regarding my father, and right there, on the plane, I think You gave it to me. Remember the strange encounter with the flight attendant? She made some offhand comments as we were disembarking about it being a good thing that we were all flying in today and not yesterday as the weather had been so bad. Everyone politely ignored her in their eagerness to disembark. I turned to her and smiled and asked her how severe the storm had been. It had been so bad, she said, that a lady had begun chanting the rosary right at the onset. And then, without thinking, I said to her:

"I bet a lot of other people were praying. Isn't it strange how in times of crisis, even atheists find God?"

She smiled. "I said my rosary too."

"Oh, are you Catholic?" I asked.

"Yes."

Then she proceeded to pull me into the back of the plane as if she were performing the most natural gesture. She gave me several fine gifts including prayer booklets and various magazines. She insisted on an author I had to read. I saw her again in the airport lobby where she gave me another gift.

Lord, You really are a secret adventurer, aren't You? You play these hide-and-seek games, and if we stopped to examine them instead of passing them off as coincidences, we would see that You are not just passively involved in our lives, but in active and exciting ways. You give us the power of interpretation and I can't help but wonder how often it has averted minor accidents and major catastrophes in our lives. Were You speaking to me in such a way when in 1997, I had a premonition about my trip to New Orleans? I'd had a dream the night before that I had been murdered there. Rising earlier than usual that morning, I sat at the kitchen table brooding about my dream and the impending trip later in the day. I was getting the feeling that I simply should not go. In the midst of my confusion and preoccupation I was startled by my mother who, ignorant of the dream and of my ambivalence about the trip, alerted me to some news report about this old lady in New Orleans making a plea to the police to stop the murders that were happening there. They were all dying there, the old woman said.

My request is that You strengthen our spirit of discernment and interpretive powers.

God:

The integral philosopher Ken Wilber says "All excellence is elitist." And why shouldn't it be? Spiritual elitism does not mean arbitrary discrimination, nor does it mean having traits others are denied. To be an elitist of the soul is to aspire to and work toward embodying the highest possible. It is the opposite of smug, narcissistic complacency in the manner of: I am the way I am and I cannot change.

I often hunger for things in this world that must seem possible only for a transcendent self. God, sometimes I must seem like an implausible character. You must wonder: *How can he be so silly. How can he hold a Ph.D. and still be so naive about the nature of what he asks for?*

If You thought so, God, You would be right. How can I ask for things that can only be purchased by a future self? But this is what spirituality means for me today, in this moment as I struggle to discover it for myself. If getting back to You means killing the self-centered and narcissistic love of the false self that is practiced in the world, then, I must try.

Everything around me is created for the sole purpose of making that self remain in existence. The cultural accoutrements that I can identify are bent on satisfying the idiosyncratic desires of that voided self—which means that they are geared toward achieving spiritual oppression. To know this and to partake in them is to be complicitous in my own oppression. If I had a strong self, there would be no need for me to live defensively and to be so easily hurt by the criticisms of others. The Narcissistic Self is a bloated mirage that exists largely on its own puffed-up gas and the addicted affirmation of others. When others poke at it, when they withhold praise, then it deflates. That's me, Lord. When suffering eats its way at my sanity because I worship the bloated self, then I look for sympathy. But is that really spiritual suffering? It seems to me that to equate privation of certain wants and desires—or worse, the contemplation of them and then refusal of the antidote—as authentic suffering, is an egregious error.

Authentic moral suffering does not consist only in grieving the loss of the old self. It is to hunger for the delayed pregnancy one experiences as one waits for years, decades even, for the birth of this elusive and precarious higher spiritual self—a new *not-yet-self*. It is to cry from joy at the possibility of having it one day and also to cry at the possibility of never completely owning it. It is to cry at the silliness of my hubris: I took the practice of the old self with its glamour and over-achieving status as the culmination of evolution. But to admit that the greatness I've longed for has eluded me is to cry at the failure of my dreams. And now, I am tired at the daunting task of the journey ahead: unlearning old habits of the old self; and adopting new strategies to disown the comfort zones that prevented taking risks.

Will the loneliness I have experienced be small compared to the loneliness that accompanies authentic transformation? This transformation, God, evidence of which we see in the lives of those who crave for makeovers on reality television shows, to those who pay for expensive eco-tourist vacations in Costa Rican rain-forests leaves me wondering if it will provide answers to these questions: Who am I, really? What do I ultimately want from this life, knowing full well that that question must be asked from the deepest and highest self? And the cry that results from this question also, Lord, is the answer that all spiritual adventurers and ar-cheologists have always been told. It is: *Cast aside everything that you are now and learn the process of forgetting where you came from.*

God:

I write again out of restlessness and a feeling of: Where is the meaning and what's the use?

It has been eight months and so much has happened, so much for which I should be thankful.

My very first book, *Becoming a Cosmopolitan: What It Means to Be a Human Being in the New Millennium* has been accepted and will be published in eight heady months. I have neglected our correspondence during all the excitement.

The excitement came, and after it passed, I felt a crawling emptiness and a maniacal urge to fill my life up. It's almost as if I want some magical omnipotence from You to ward off the maniacal feeling of cosmic meaninglessness and emptiness. I am disappointed with success. It's not like I imagined it would be at all. I thought publishing my first book, and doing the radio interviews, and giving my first lecture in Europe—all of which I did enjoy—would fill me up. I thought the pride I felt would be enough.

Nothing is enough. The void opens up even more and I am swallowed up in oceans of incompleteness.

Now that the years of struggling to get published are over, my body tells me to rest but I am impelled to push on, to feel filled up.

Dear God:

How should I learn to pray? I dream of a more exalted and triumphant self. But at this moment I am what I am. I am not content to remain what I am. I desire change. But how to work with what I have now? Teach me, dear God, how to approach You honorably from the highest and purest standpoint of who I am now. None of it can be faked. I cannot feign a self I do not have; I cannot utter words in the manner of the Self I am yet to become. That would be miming.

As I write this, I feel You inspiring me once more, to ask You for a new approach to the nature of suffering. We've all given it a bad name, seen it as something to be remedied via therapy and pills. I have not had the courage to see it as a firm invitation to look at what I am actually *being* in my daily life. I am not seeing this suffering as an invitation to live a more inwardly expansive life; to plunge the interiors of the soul rather than allow it to be hijacked by glibness, greed, laziness, and moral cowardice.

Propel me into Your divine light and let me think not to equate the tribulations of the ego-driven self as the source of real suffering.

Restore in us veneration for noble suffering. Give us the grace of those who have suffered honorably, knowing that the spiritual replenishment wrought thereof, dwarfs the shallow rewards yearned for by the old self.

Implant in our midst the likeness of Your spiritual heroes and giants—great specimens of Your humanity, who, for just a moment can inspire us, cajole us, and show us the magnitude of all that which is possible.

My Dearest God:

It has been a while since I wrote to you. Well over a month. It seems like I have been too busy for You, too busy with the minutiae of my life, and too busy with the big dreams and ambitions.

Oh, God, walking this morning in the park I felt Your presence so deeply in my life. I felt You surrounding me and enveloping me in all Your love and sweetness. I am so happy. I had felt like I lost You, like You had slipped through my hands again. I spoke last week to my aunt of not feeling Your presence and not feeling close to You. But this morning, as I looked at the lake and felt the last vestige of winter shrug its blasts across my face, I felt You!

I felt Your presence as I reminisced about my past in which You were deeply denied. And as I walked, I was humbled and felt a bit ashamed because even in my unconscious anger against You, You were still guiding my life and sending me closer to the destiny that awaits me.

You gave me the strength of conviction even when my mind was not focused on You. You gave them to me because You knew that the intensity of the convictions was needed to sustain me, and that that intensity would redirect itself in the service of a new set of moral beliefs and principles. And so, I return once more to commune with You and to ask You for grace. I am asking for something that I do not fully understand, but I know that it is not something that I ought to pray for, or should I? How does one get grace? These are the questions to which I seek answers. As always, once I start writing to You, my meditation lapses into tangential thinking. But what I really wanted, God, was to thank You for the gift of Your presence this morning. Perhaps it was what stirred the desire to feel the nature of the question about grace. You filled me with your presence without me asking for it.

Thank You.

Dear God:

I've been thinking about the slowness of my relationship with you, how at times there appears to be little continuity between one intimate encounter with You and another. I feel I know Your presence in my work as a philosopher. I sense Your voice and Your density as I write and move between the worlds of reason and faith. Reason guides my arguments, but faith saturates the premises I feel are true.

To write on behalf of mankind and to advocate its unification is to write about the love that You have for all of us, but which we pervert by idolizing the surface dimensions that cover the hearts and souls. So, a legitimate question for You: Why permit surface qualities such as skin color and the shape of a chin to be used to dehumanize others?

This issue is considered trite by many—unfortunately. But I deeply feel that it comes back to the lessons we must learn in order to morally evolve. In the same way that personhood is an achievement, so moral maturity is an achievement and a prerequisite for a share in the Divine Life that we genetically inherit from You.

It is becoming increasingly clear that moral philosophy is a way for me to achieve moral maturity. The gifts You gave me are resources that are not meant to be indulged in only for my personal satisfaction. *The gifts must be used to cultivate a new humanity that is the inheritance of all of humankind.*

And so, my prayer to You is this: *Continue using me as a vehicle to serve the highest ends of humankind.* Continue giving me the strength to move in faith and listen, listen carefully to the many ways in which you speak to me. God, I think this is difficult. It seems as if You sometimes use fools and idiots to deliver a message. Afterwards, it becomes a sort of test.

Authentic idiots are the ones who cannot discern the pearls of wisdom contained in the speech of the fool. And when I am able to do this, I understand it as the challenging process of witnessing humanity in all humans. Hope is alive because even the foolish have the capacity to point the way of truth.

My voice is still secular. But my heart is groping for a spiritual and religious sensibility. This is a form of spiritual schizophrenia is it not, to speak one way but to dream of speaking in another, to have one's thoughts be mediated by anger and vanity, and to know by the heart that there is another way, and that it is the right way?

Again, God, I am praying for moral wisdom.

God:

The late novelist Toni Morrison says that writing stretches the individual and takes a person to the borders of him or herself. I feel this way in chasing You. It's as if I'm chasing an elusive would-be lover who leaves marks everywhere, but I am either too fatigued or blind to identify the clues.

I am being stretched to my limits in my capability to feel You, to know You. That's just the way it feels, sometimes. I'm not declaring this as gospel truth. How do I learn once more to live from the deepest center of who I am? Where is that center? Beyond the abyss I stare into, and dream of falling inside to lose myself? Forever. That abyss is more real than even my breath blown into my palms.

This never-ending loneliness is back to plague me. I know I sound like a stuck record, but isn't that what the eternal drama of the human condition seems to be? All the themes and patterns keep repeating in our lives and we chant: The demons are back to haunt us again; the demons are back.

A gifted songwriter says that there is a crack in everything, and that is how the light gets in.

God, If I crack open a little wider, will you let some of your light in?

How does one really talk to You? Find You? Is it through religion? In churches? Synagogues? Mosques? Temples? Is it through love? But look at love. It devastates the heart, it breaks us to pieces, and it drives us to mold ourselves into shapes that make us unrecognizable to ourselves and to those whom we love. Not always. But too often to feel safe in its eternal promises. Then again, there is the beauty in love. I look at my mother caring for my grandmother, and I worry that at the end of her vigil that she might not be able to recover a personal life for herself. Will she emerge whole at the end of it all? Will she lose her sanity, will it wear her down, or will the experience take her to a sacred place?

What is the real root of loneliness God? And why has it been the loyal companion of so many? How do we eradicate it from our hearts?

And now, the big question.

What if You decide not to grant grace? What if You decide to let me be a wandering itinerant for the rest of my life, filled with philosophical passion but void of the fullness of being that I crave?

I have often said that I write in order to become the person I would most like to be. And as I write these letters to you, I write to become a ritualized devotee of all that You are. Are the people who say that all one has to do is accept Christ, and God will enter your life liars? Last night I had the instant magical feeling of being in Your presence. I went to bed with the words, *I had a talk with Jesus,* on my lips.

Sometimes I wonder if Buddhists are correct in preaching emptiness: no attachments, no desire, and no deep wants. They say these are all the roots of suffering and that the recipe for a blissful life consists in removing them from our lives. But to remove desire, needs, and attachments—the basis for our emotional ties in the world that make us distinctly human—would be to react from fear. We fear the loss of a loved one, therefore we must ensure that we never depend on that person for our happiness. We love that person in some alien impersonal way. But we are not closed systems. We need others. And we need our complicated relationships with them to negotiate the arduous task of exploring and constructing our humanity. We have to admit, God, that it is in the uncertainty of knowing whether our personal love will take us to the brink of despair, or to states of exaltation that we find the strength to exhume our buried seeds of life. This we call *Vital Life.*

Love is not an admission of certainty about how we will feel about our chosen mates twenty years from the declaration of dependency that is made when we say: *I love you.* It is a commitment made more in the nobility of intention, than in the certainty of where that love will lead us. We are creatures in need of love and dependency. Those who decry this attachment repress their own cosmic dependency. So, what does it mean to evacuate ourselves from attachments?

It would require us to evacuate the self of many of the concrete experiences that make us heartbreakingly human: the first smile on the face of one's child; the way the face of a loved one unfolds slowly like a rose petal at the sight of puppy frolicking with its bone, tossing it up this way and that way and then gnawing at it while both its forelegs, crossed furtively like two hands, cover its pittance of a used-up treasure and looks up with solemn eyes towards those of its owner who cannot move, and who cannot bear to stand still. Transfixed. Awed by the focused, loving attention the puppy dedicates to its gift of the day. The owner is mesmerized by the spectacle of a creature living in the now. The owner of the dog is transcendentally buoyed, and that feeling of transcendence will be a memory to her mind in the weeks, months and, perhaps, decades ahead. How does she evacuate herself from that deep exquisite emotion? Isn't that one tiny detail, Lord, an imperceptible moment of the sublime where You sometimes reside? Suffering finds a palliative moment in that memory of a puppy so focused on its gift. And rather than wondering where the glory is, where is the exalted moment in which she can find magic and ascribe it to You, she sees instead, a small creature, living, being in its world, incapable of questioning. The owner of this delicate creature imputes goodness to that puppy, and in that space between fantasy and need, Your presence settles around her, softly. And the only evidence she has is that she feels unexplainable calmness. And she never wants to leave that feeling. She simply settles into it.

Help me, God, to distinguish among the different types of suffering: the self-indulgent and narcissistic suffering which I inflict on myself in order to gain authority over others; the suffering that comes from the loss of the material things I need in my life to make me whole; the things I mourn for because I have not grown used to their absence from my life; and the suffering I inflict on others out of spite, anger, fear, and insecurity. These are all logical forms of suffering caused by self-inflicted soul damage.

Above all, Lord, help me not to be afraid of *Enlightened Suffering*—the suffering from which I draw moral lessons, the suffering that stretches my soul and reconfigures my humanity, the suffering that leaves me with expanded moral realities and the vision of a spirit I couldn't have conjured on my own.

This is what the artist and the life-affirming creative impulses in the human heart have tried to capture: to bring into existence the pieces of our spirit that You left for us to craft on our own.

God:

I'm trying to understand how we love when we love, and to reconcile the tensions inherent in how I love and the idea of a pure love, (assuming there is such a thing).

How do I know that my love really is love rather than the weight of emotional baggage laden with illusions? Perhaps all love is mediated by emotional baggage. We love with the weight of the woes of our characters that drag us to the ground as we find places to deposit them—in experience, in addictions, in work and in play, and in the lives of those whom we love. Hardly a healthy recipe. But perhaps we ameliorate our strained practices of love through these painful mediations and learn from the lessons they visit upon us. The more cracked our souls are, the more the light gets in.

God, I feel that my relationships are like archeological field trips I take into the world—only, the soil being unearthed and ploughed is my own. I feel I have become more healed and more whole as a result of my relationships, and that I could not have done it on my own.

Dear God:

Want to know what I have learned from writing to You?

That the myths I held at the beginning of these letters were not empowering myths. They were rationalizations I coined to make sense of my unhappiness.

That holding such beliefs meant I had to sacrifice my humanity in certain realms, to live in the future, to deny the present and the small pleas they made on my life for the simplest of pleasures, and that had more to do with the dread of realizing my humanity to its fullest, than with accomplishment. I know now that my humanity has to be conceived in union with the authentic demands of my soul and the conviction that I, with my flaws, am worthy of happiness.

That voices of wisdom and insight come in different ways. Therefore, we should exercise awareness of the places we visit, the people we spend our time with, and where it is that we think our place in the world is.

That for me home is not where the action is, or where I feel titillated, rather, it is where calmness and equanimity exist and where serenity finds me despite my high-strung nature. Home is the peace that finds me when I think there is no peace in the world—like the calm bedroom of my grandmother. There she lies, paralyzed and speechless, but she winks and smiles at me from the bottom of her beautiful soul.

Many thanks to you, God, for driving my soul to seek home.

Dearest God:

Five years have passed, and I am yet to keep this date with You. Five years have passed, and I have lost my beloved grandmother, suffered nervous breakdowns, hospitalizations, and devastating panic attacks. Five years have passed and still, in this insufferable void, there is blood, despair, and the cry of the Death Baby who longs for extinction and feels nostalgia for its eviction from the womb. Crumpled into a state of inert wormhood, the baby blindly gropes for a return to the womb that is not a womb, but a makeshift tomb. When I try to speak to Death Baby, I am at a loss for words. It is inconsolable. It is a black hole. It cries out from where it is drowning inside the void: *Oh, God, how I want to die. Oh God, please let me die.* Who is this child and who conjured up its life deep inside of me? I taste the saltiness on its lips, dream that its lungs will turn to gills so that it won't die. And then, I begin to cry. When I seek the solace of You and of Your presence, I simply cannot find You. And from the blood in that void, there is nowhere to swim to. I cannot tread any longer. And still, You are not there.

I carry the cross, the beautiful golden cross that I flash before the eyes of airport security agents, the cross that sits atop my laptop and that dark place deep, deep inside my pants pocket. Not a day goes by that I leave home without it. I carry You, and You rest against my leg.

Oh God, this search and this journey back to You is my life's goal. I have given up the childish desire to be zapped, to be struck by Your lightening rod, which is to say nothing more than: Give me grace!

If I can still pen my words to You, if I may believe that the will to pray lies not in my voice so much as it does in my fingers, then there is a way to find You. Evolution and moral becoming are my goals—not conversion. To seek my way to You is to continue the journey of reconstructing my humanity through my fellow human beings. I admit: They terrify me. I admit the flight into my profession, my writing, and my scholarship has as much to do with hiding from humanity as it does with trying to love it.

I know the rat inside of me cannot come out unless I admit that there is a rat inside of me, a gnawing pestilential rat that, for some reason, I have wanted to kill. Was my anger at You, God, anger that for some strange, strange reason, you never annihilated the Death Baby in me I cannot bring myself to kill? A Death Baby who can live only if I memorialize it by torturing it by overkill: achievement, glory, love, love, and love and trying to atone for the sin of simply existing? I exist. And for existing I feel such shame. Sometimes I mumble to myself like an old woman: *I do not want to be here. I do not want to be here.* And then, when nausea takes over and I am sick of my own consciousness, I shake my fist skyward where I imagine You reclining in leisure, and I hiss: *I don't want to be here.* The pain of existence becomes a prolongation of futile living when I feel this unwanted truth: Nothing in the finite sphere of the humanly created can ever extract the poison inside of me; only You can take it away.

Last night I slept on my back, waiting for that kiss on my forehead from You that I dreamed could extract the poison.

I own my betrayal of You. I own the freedom I sought in walking away. You never pushed me. You never abandoned me. I shall never call what I did hubris, nor shall I regret it.

I have come to know the depths of my deepest humanity in disclaiming You, and I have come to know the abyss, the terror, and the darkness that entombs one when radical freedom leaves one anchored to nothing but one's own free-falling imagination. It falls, falls, and falls into eternal bottomless space. This is *my* terror, Lord. And this is the darkness. This is the freedom that I chose. This was the kingdom I made. And this was the kingdom I inherited from my own will.

There is eternal dignity in that freedom and a gracious autonomy that I could not have traded.

What is the answer, God? Give me a sign, give me a sign I keep saying to You almost every day, as if You haven't already given me enough.

Where exactly are You located, God. I mean, address, telephone number, and email?

Where are Your footprints buried? Under trampled sand that only a rabid dog could have the sense to sniff out? Show me so I may follow them wherever they lead, even back to starvation in a desert where, through redemption, I can find fulfillment in a real place, a real space and where I can be anchored back to a tethered imagination that need not find a space outside of Your will, Your thoughts.

Lord, there is no freedom in my mind.

Only darkness; darkness and a never-ending free-fall.

Dear God:

So many, many years have passed. My pursuit of you has continued quietly. I have ceased documenting it in letters.

I have now written now five books, lectured all across Europe and the United States and Asia, and I have achieved some modicum of recognition as a public intellectual having appeared on several television and radio and podcast broadcasts. I write for several major magazines and no longer covet fame and glory. I seek only to fortify Your name. To play my part in unifying humankind; to help people recognize our common humanity that transcends the arbitrariness of race, ethnicity, and nationality. I have been censured and rebuked by my university for defending Israel and Jewish civilization as a Christian. I have been strengthened in the infliction of cruelty against me by Your love and deep abiding presence.

The aching loneliness has left me. I have grown deeper into Your presence and given my life to you. Your plentitude fills me up in a way I had not thought imaginable. Over the years my prayer life has grown stronger and stronger. When I felt You were not there, I simply spoke to You out loud, knowing, of course, that You were and are always by my side. Everything I have asked of You, You have granted me.

Now I find myself in the position of caring for my mother who is slowly dying of cancer. I find myself outside of my life. It feels that way. I am grounded by Your love; yet I feel discombobulated in having to return to Jamaica for nine months to care for her after having left the country thirty-eight years ago. I follow Your lead in everything.

My return to You in letters feels as organic and natural as if I had just written to You yesterday; and that is because for the last fifteen years I have cultivated a different self though Your grace and love.

Dear God:

Over twenty years ago when I began writing these letters to You, I spoke of shame and guilt. And in that space, I was even too ashamed and guilty to confess to you about what we spoke of between the lines. As much as I made myself vulnerable and transparent, I fooled myself into thinking I could not face You with the deepest source of joy and anguish that had befallen me in like. Joy because I found love in that state for almost fourteen years; anguish because I am now convinced it is an affliction that tears me in two.

So, what is the source of this affliction?

This same-sex attraction that has now left me bereft. I grow more convinced as I adduce my life as evidence that You did not create gay people, that they were not born that way. Rather, a set of existential circumstances formed those afflicted. For years I thought You made me this way from when I was in the womb. Despite a happy relationship with Fred for almost fourteen years—this affliction, since that relationship ended, has brought me nothing but anguish and heartbreak. I see the moral bankruptcy, the idolatry, and the emptiness at the epicenter of gay culture. The entire culture centers around carnality and lust, promiscuity, drugs, and worship at the altar of the cult of beauty and youth.

I cannot be a part of that culture. I was proudly gay. I held that identity as central to my identity. I cannot be a part of that culture. It is decadent and rotten to the core. I cannot identify as gay anymore. I can say I am a same-sex attracted person, but as You know Lord, I am in a quandary: celibate and chaste because it feels right, but lonely at times for the simple warmth of companionship. I hear Your voice, and I feel You pulling me away from this way of living. I heed Your call, because it is just, and because it is right.

I never asked for this affliction. If I could change my orientation, You know I would God. So, I have asked You to weaken my attraction to men—and You have. The insatiable hunger and maniacal desire to find fulfilment in a same-sex relationship has left me. Hallelujah! I asked You to complete me and fulfil me. And you have. Blessed are those lonely souls living in inequity who cry out to you for some relief, and gratitude to You who soothed the desperate cries of the afflicted.

But the source of the affliction. I know now it did not come from You. Why have I waited for almost fifty-four years to name the terrible day when my soul was crushed, my body violated, my mouth bruised. I was six years old. How could You? Why did You leave me in his hands, pinned under his body. Helpless. Guilty. Ashamed. The taste of blood in my mouth for days. And I was only six years old.

God:

In this moment I am invoking You to be a witness by my side as I remember; to hold me in that remembered space, and to keep me held.

The picture is clear in your mind. My grandfather's estate. Yallas, Jamaica. I am six years old. The workhands are all men and adolescent boys. I trusted him. Tony was his name. I am in my brown leather sandals, and overall shorts. He is holding my hands as if he were taking me to church. He is leading me down a path towards the beach. Only we are about a hundred yards from the beach. There is an embankment, a trench. It looks like the trenches the soldiers in WWII used to hunker down in to hide from the enemies and fire their shots. I am not afraid. He has always been kind to me and my brother. The sand is cold and soothing as he places me on my stomach. He is on top of me, grinding and writhing himself against my back. My clothes are on. He does not remove them. But I feel something hard pressing into me through my clothing. Something hard and stiff. He turns me over. He lies on top of me and continues to press himself into my body, pressing it into the sand. Then he wraps his arms around me and sticks his tongue in my mouth and kisses me. His tongue is deep inside my mouth and licking my face. He tastes of blood.

My grandmother's car pulls up in the driveway way, way up ahead in the open garage. He pulls me deeper into the trench. I do not speak. I am still not afraid. I know this is wrong. We are hiding from my grandmother. Why are we hiding? He whispers into my ear not to tell anyone. Then after my grandmother has gone in the house, he lies on top of me and begins kissing me again. He buries his tongue inside my little mouth. His thick lips seem to swallow up my entire face. That's how it feels.

Next morning as I am being bathed, I feel the taste of him in my mouth. My mouth tastes of blood. It would taste that way for days to come. I could not rid myself of the taste of blood. I lived in terror my grandmother would know. That everyone would know I must have done something bad. I felt ashamed. Guilty. But Tony was so kind and gentle with us. He was always throwing me and my brother up in the air, and just as I felt as if I was going to hit the ground, he caught me, hugged me, and laughed.

This child is confused.

My next memory. I am wearing a navy-blue pair of shorts and a navy-blue little T-shirt. I am standing in the vestibule of my grandfather's bedroom looking at myself in the floor length mirror.

I am watching myself die. I have a pulled a transparent plastic bag over my face. I am suffocating and gasping for air. I watch my contorted features in the mirror. I am beginning to cry. And then Your invisible hand must have appeared. I rip the bag from my face and fall to the ground in sobs. I am six years old. When I cannot cry anymore, exhausted I go down to the beach and sit on the old, rusted fence beyond which I am forbidden to cross. I wonder when my mother and father will come back from America.

I begin to set fires inside the house. Later on, after my parents came back, divorced from each other, my father tells me that his girlfriend told him that I was setting fires inside the house because I was a homosexual who was trying to destroy himself. I am eight years old. In that moment I want to die.

I look around for a plastic bag for solace—for the solace that will come later. I cannot find one. I feel ashamed. I want the earth to open up and swallow me. I want to return to nothing. I am nothing. My heart races. I feel terribly sad. My father said those words as if he were repeating some interesting piece of news item. I am eight years old.

There is nothing more I can say or do in this letter to reveal the depths of despair and humiliation I felt. My redemptive identity was pinned on being a new surrogate child husband for my mother who was not yet thirty. She leaned on me for solace. I, the deputized stand-in for my father who had destroyed her life, and whose absence would chart the course of my future life. Promises were made. That I would never leave her. My smile lit up her depressed life. I and only I could make her happy by saying the right thing, by doing the right thing, by preempting her mood. I felt loving another woman would be a betrayal of her and that, maybe, she would not love me anymore.

And you were there, God. And in those moments I felt close to You—in some strange way. A good Catholic boy serving at the altar. But it was not there where I felt close to You. It was in solitude. Alone. Cut off from a world where there were no prying eyes. In a world in which no one wanted to be my friend. The taste of blood occasionally saturated my mouth. Could they tell?

Loneliness is like being in a room alone and then realizing that room has expanded into the whole world, and no one sees you. But I found a corner on the most deserted and barren register in my soul. I found the void. And I waited, I waited. In that moment I waited as I would wait for my father in the ensuing years when he left again. I waited in that empty space. I waited to see Your face, or to feel You with invisible arms around my shoulder. I waited for the Touch. And I began, at eight years old, to walk in the street in the middle of the night. And I raised my cup of bad, bad blood to you—Lord of the Mirrors. Atonement was behind me. Righteousness outpaced me. I walked in mourning, and I walked in solitude. Still awaiting my life which was not yet born. And still awaiting my death.

That, as of yet:

Silence.

Silence.

Silence.

And I thought You had overslept; or something like that.

Father God:

I seek You and feel at times You have divorced yourself from the world, taken a hiatus because the world has offended You, the world hurts You. So, I had this vision that Your divorce was imminent. I dreamt that You said You couldn't cry anymore because Your tear ducts had all dried up; and the farmers below watched their crops retreat into their beginnings, saw the tall blades of hay waltzing in an orgy of abandon–the last dance that never was. And then they died.

You said You couldn't stop coughing anymore because You now had asthma and smelling salts never worked. And the animals felt achy and weak, dogs kept panting, their red tongues dangling like perverted old trolls, and the air became hot and putrid, and the dogs mated with the cats, and the offspring came out with eyes of mud and bit ravenous holes from hidden teeth into the bellies of their mothers.

You said You couldn't sneeze anymore because You were all stuffed up, and winter came and never turned to spring, bees flew up, up, up into the sky thirsting, and fell back to earth in the open mouths of the children of the cats and the dogs who believed it was sinful not to wait on you, God, to provide the food they needed to sustain life within.

You said You couldn't urinate anymore because Your bladder was too thin. And there was howling on earth, the animals laughed and watched babies talk while the big people swallowed their tongues—the pure whites of their eyes swelled and bellowed and hissed, and flies laid their eggs upon these snowy mountains.

You said You couldn't remember how to breathe because You were losing your memory. And silence fell upon the earth. The swollen whites heaved and sighed, and the eggs of the flies burst open, blackness filled the skies shielding them like armories of gilded mosaics. The howling ceased; the bees stopped falling. Bodies rotted and swelled and hissed like little pressure cookers.

God, You said You were going to sleep, because You were grouchy and tired. Your face moved over waters of the earth making the sign of the cross, from the

Caribbean Sea to the Adriatic Sea, the Indian Ocean to the Pacific. But the Earth had already tilted off its axis, falling, falling into the great void.

God, You said You didn't want to wake up, because You had no reason to. But there was no one there to hear You—only vast emptiness that absorbed nothing. So, You thought You had lost Your voice. And You dreamed of children playing ring around the rosie in a tiny garden that You created long ago.

God:

I am still working through the process of contemplating You. If it becomes a psychological enterprise, that is contemplating the consciousness of my own conscious sense of who You are, then it becomes a contemplation of my own consciousness, and of the codified concepts of You that have accrued in my mind. It all becomes self-referential because the object of my contemplation is my mediated consciousness of myself contemplating You.

I believe the antidote in contemplating lies above consciousness. In those moments of contemplation, I will need to dissolve my consciousness and dive into the mystery of your being. There, I shall find the yet-to-be-named presence that enshrouds me. This cannot be apprehended by consciousness. This experience is a *supersedence* of consciousness. It is entrance into Your plentitude of being, Your loving presence, Your will. It becomes an enmeshment experience where the boundaries between me and the presence of You are indistinguishable. Not co-dependence. Reciprocal co-habitation. My presence co-mingled and then pressed into Yours. This is the antithesis of alienation. This is the ground of all being.

Father:

If there is a creating spirit of You that dwells inside us, and if we also dwell inside of You, then what happens to you Lord, when those who dwell in You commit their moral depredations and putrefaction in You? What symptoms do our moral depredations and opprobrium elicit in You?

I have a vision planted in me by You that tragedies, afflictions, pain, and suffering are the expulsions of our depravity that we commit as we dwell in You. The result is codified chaos. We all have free will and You simply empty Yourself of our exercise of that free will back into the world. Each one of us as we dwell in You is turned back upon the world and set loose. Pain and suffering are the ways we are held accountable for the evisceration of ourselves in that sacred dwelling place inside of You. Your purity is an embarrassment to the conflicted desires we harbor. We flee the dwelling place to pursue our freedom. We evict ourselves from the only source of moral freedom and traverse the abyss, the chaos, the contradictory.

And then, lost and no longer feeling as one of Your kind, we pin our redemptive identity on a contrite return to the dwelling place we evicted ourselves from.

God:

Now I am in search of You again. I am anxious and afraid that I have lost You. I must have faith that You are still right by my side. Your presence is not a feeling. It is an occupancy You take up inside me that is always there. I must discern multiple ways of witnessing the occupancy as opposed to becoming obsessed with having a feeling of Your presence. You can't be experienced in psychological categories. My restlessness today, and my anxiety do not constitute proof of your absence. Psychological states of fullness or absence are not proof of your presence or absence. Psychological states of frustration are not sufficient to go on a search for You. There is no search because You never went anywhere. If I had resided in hope, rather than in presence-in-waiting, I would have seen You.

I must bear witness and honor the multitude of ways in which you manifest Yourself in the world. I must find You as you materialize in the world: as a *series of possibilities* that always avail themselves to humanity. You are multitudinous. This disclosure of possibilities that reveal themselves as opportunities for me to grow fuller in the image in which You made me is also a vocational calling. A calling to find myself in solidarity with others, in community, in vulnerability, in embarrassment, humiliation, and rejection, in hope and love—in all manners of being human; in the ways that Christ himself navigated the world. In these possibilities that I manifest through my actions and, therefore, my agency, I find original assemblages of You as You are, and as I could be, and as I ought to be.

The lost and disassembled parts of ourselves that we have dislodged from our being are found in Your disclosures. We piece back together the wholesome and fulsome image we started out with but discarded through sin and neglect, via moral laxity, that resulted in spiritual atrophy. These disclosures are not always apparently attractive to the egoic self.

Still, we take them on in faith and hope, in moral certainty, that the reconstruction of the soul requires the dying of the old self and its false expectations.

God:

I believe therapists when they say that narcissism is one of the most difficult personality disorders to treat. In contemplation, I realize that it cannot be remedied psychologically. The only way I, or anyone else can escape the poison of narcissism is to empty myself completely of my desires and needs and wants. To stop the performance that elicits the narcissistic fuel from others that feeds my void. I must be open to the design of You upon my soul. The imprimatur of Your love that already resides in me. I must seek to feel myself loved in a new way. To see the ways in which Christ reveals his love in me through the virtuous lovingness of others. I must learn to break with others; those whose toxic love I have grown addicted to; those who feed me a false image of myself that reinforces a bloated egocentric sense of who I take myself to be.

But what does it mean to learn to love others from a Christ-centric perspective, and, concomitantly, to only accept the love from others who love from a Christ-centric perspective?

It means realizing that I need only be. I need only to exist in order to be loved by You. That I love You and honor You, that I need not predicate my worth on worldly success and achievement and become an accomplishment addict to feel worthy of love. That I cultivate my Christ-spirit and manifest it in the world, and that my love from that space is among the highest of my callings. The Holy Spirit living in the depths of my heart is the same Holy Spirit living in the depths of the hearts of my brothers and sisters. How could any of us feel the despairing loneliness and emptiness that calls out the narcissists to create a false grandiose self that craves love based on worldly achievements when the most magnanimous lover—Christ—dwells in each heart? He yearns to be summoned. In like manner, He would have us practice as spiritual lovers to each other—the personal spiritual lover He is to us. Can we return to others the love Christ feels for us? A repetitive cycle of reciprocated love?

God:

Today, once again I am paralyzed by anxiety. Utterly paralyzed. Writing to You has become a painful task. I cannot sense You. I do not feel calm. I do not feel Your presence. You are absent. A million miles away. I feel like a gutted and empty fish tossed on a riverbank gasping for air. I feel utterly abandoned and alone. For weeks I felt at one with You, felt the peace with which You are flooding my body and my soul. I want so badly to discontinue writing these letters. I am racked with doubt. Can I do this properly? I'm at a loss for how to speak to You. Where are You? Is this a test of faith? To feel Your absence and void but to still pursue You and seek You relentlessly? To write in the midst of the void. To hope for equanimity and peace of mind? I fear revealing the personal.

Why? Why do I fear it?

Because deep down inside I feel that I am nothing. An insignificant piece of scrap on the earth. I fear that I will reveal the extent to which I must reveal the depths to which I must justify my existence and prove to myself that I have objectively justified my existence.

I fear writing from the heart. I am all armor on the outside, encased in kryptonite. Inside the strength and valor are there, and yet, there is a man without skin and membrane, sensitive and perceptive—too perceptive, without the cataracts of illusions.

Prayer for Those Who Feel Distant from God and Anxious:

Lord, though we are, indeed, like scattered lambs on some distant patch, and though through our blettings and cries we cannot console each other—for now—while we look for You so close by: Let us find the compassion in our hearts to bring solace and tenderness to each other.

It might be quite a while before we feel like we find You. But we lost lambs have each other. We forge a bond in the crucibles of loneliness and anxiety. We feel loneliness and anxiety are infectious, so the bond is often fractured. We distract ourselves from getting together. We seek you in isolation. Not knowing that You and Your presence are everywhere. Not in some isolated spot.

Lord, give me the wisdom and courage to turn to see the person next to me in line at the supermarket. And while You seem so far away, let me see the shape of Your smile printed on her face. Give me simple surety of heart to brave it and tell another of the nakedness of my pain and anxiety. Give me the sense of trusting vulnerability to tell another what it feels like to have found You and, to feel that panic when You feel like mercury slipping through my fingers and are gone. And in some way, I, too, am gone.

Give me the courage to hold the conviction that abandonment of your children is alien to who You are. Let me hold that conviction as my heart races, my palms sweat, and I feel locked inside a tight room. Let the thought of Your steady soothing presence quiet my mind. Let me remember such moments as I had. Give me a sense of humor, too, Lord. To look upon myself and laugh at the irony of *knowing* that you are sitting so close by my side, and yet I remain oblivious to Your presence. Let me laugh and know why I am laughing: to see if Your laughter is so loud and uproarious in response to mine that one has to go deaf to hear remnants and vibrations in Your voice.

In those anxious moments when I am paralyzed, Lord, breathe with me. As I inhale, let me feel the intake of Your breath with mine. Let a surge of peace rush to my head, my lungs, my hands and feet and toes. Let me exhale compassion, relief, sadness, and doubt and know that You are returning to my soul with my next breath.

Lord:

As I listen to Gregorian chants, I'm not sure why I'm weeping. But I know there is this great longing to be filled up by You; an aching void that opened up again today accompanied by a deep love for You. I feel inconsolable. I cannot identify the source of my grief. I only know anything less than the fullness of Your being in my soul feels unbearable; as if I cannot be suited for life on earth, for this world unless I can almost taste You and feel You coursing through my veins. This is an obsession and an indulgence. You are more than that? Please help me to transcend the materiality of my desire and need for the physicality of Your Being. It's too much. I feel like an addict looking for a high. A God-high. But is that pursuit such a bad thing? I am celibate. I don't do drugs. I rarely imbibe. I have a human body. I am a corporeal entity. Is it not natural, then, that I should crave exaltation and an implacable desire for the highest possible? Is it not natural to need to feel it in real time, in the corporeal dimensions of my body, and other reaches of my spirit? Show me other ways.

God:

As I care for my mother here in Jamaica as she suffers from stage 4 cancer of the breast I am amazed at the equanimity, the patience, the fortitude, and acceptance that have all befallen me as I try to nurse her. I thank You Lord, that in giving up my life in the USA to come to Jamaica to care for her that I have not fallen prey to resentment, upset, and depression over her plight. My own spiritual plight and yearning for You is of a different nature. I thank You for sparing her life when one dose of chemotherapy almost killed her. The ravages of cancer and the omnipresence of death given the weakened state of her heart draws me closer to You. You are the Great Eternal Hope. All my desires in the word may fail except one: the desire to be loved by You. I know that there is an infallibility affixed to that desire. I may waver in my love for You. You will never reciprocate that inconstancy in my love for You.

I have my brother whose wife was battling with her own advanced cancer for six weeks and has now died. So, in one way if my mother dies—you're all I have left. Just as in her mind, I am all that she has left in the world.

I was looking for glory in the wrong places: in achievements and worldly success, even in the cultivation of moral virtues in my character. There is only one place to see eternal glory and exaltation and that is in the space in our soul where God has already placed it. I have had the traumatic experience of weaning myself from this material attachment to earthly and worldly glory.

I have been deeply hurt by a friend who was part of my inner circle; a trusted confidante who, out of jealousy, trivialized and made fun of my academic achievements, one of my prestigious academic titles. The nasty comments, the ridicule cut to the bone. This was someone whom I trusted and admired and had looked up to since I was a young adolescent. This person had been like a father figure to me since I was sixteen years old. I suppose the affirmation and validation that I once needed still lingers unconsciously. I felt humiliated and betrayed—deeply so.

This person also sexually fondled me within weeks of meeting me. He was the husband of my mother's best friend. At seventeen he forced his hands down my shorts and fondled me. I did not resist. I could not. How do you resist the advances of the only man that has acted as your father when your only father has abandoned you and left you to die an emotional death? He got me addicted to the idea of homosexuality as pursuit of the lost father. I lived in an emotionally confusing and painful stage of life.

He made me feel as if I would never be lonely again. It was around that time I stopped praying. A creeping agnosticism lay in wait for me just around the corner.

All male same-sex cultures, wherever they exist in the world—exist in an insatiable lust for constant sex. Carnality and an insatiable drive for addictive sex are the constitutive features of gay life.

Prayer For Those Who Feel Unheard by Others,
Who Seek a Deep Emotional Connection:

Dear Lord:

We live in a country in which people are suffering from what psychologists call an *epidemic of loneliness*. Never in our history as a species have more people committed suicide, taken prescription drugs for depression and anxiety; never in our history have more people complained of feeling disconnected from their fellow compatriots. People complain of a void when around others, that others just do not get them, and that they are not heard when they speak. They are psychologically invisible before others. Alienation and anxiety exacerbate their feeling of being abandoned in and to the world.

If you are that person, I share your suffering. I have been that person. On occasion I still am.

Lord, I have found that one way out of the morass of loneliness that periodically afflicts me is truly understanding one of Your commandments: to love thy neighbor as thyself. This is not an ego-based sentimental or transactional love. It is to love You, God, in my neighbor as I love you—the eternal God—that resides in me.

Our loneliness is fueled by transitory and ephemeral desires that change with people's moods and fluctuating interests. I exist in a state of perpetual anxiety as I wear masks, play endless roles, and manufacture images of myself to coax and seduce others into satisfying my egoic needs.

For the people who are suffering from loneliness and disconnection from others, teach them to understand that it is not until they love the immutable and non-changing source in others—the Christ within—that they will feel the abundance of Your presence shining in their souls.

Help them, Lord, to find the omnipresence of Christ in their souls, the Eternal Father they have in You that they first must honor. When we do this, we learn to hold on to, in any human being in the world, the single thread that unites us in a common unity with You, God. We find oneness in our commiseration with others. The connection we feel is not some superficial psychological affinity with others. It is not some lust for just emotional intimacy with another, which, in the end, will always lead us to suffering.

I pray, Lord, that the lonely and alienated will locate the Divine Eternal Love You have for us within themselves, and know that through their presentation in the world, they are representatives of the Christ within them. Others get to know us in the manner that we allow our Christly love You present within us to be directed to them: those whom we know, and also the stranger, the foreigner—the adversary. I pray that when those of us in times of doubt, find it hard to locate that love residing in us, that we be lit by a spark others ignite in us as they open us in Christly love to You.

I pray that through their sacred presence we see the Divine. The *mysterium* is no more. You are not shrouded in darkness anymore. I pray that we are almost blinded by that love of You they feel for us. May we be washed in peace and equanimity. May we be left with the implacable certainty in knowing that that love lives and breathes inside of us. Give us all the courage to exhale that love as life support for others who are cast into the dustbin of history—lonely, dejected, unheard, and invisible. Give those on the brink of giving up the desire to inhale that love and breathe it out only for us to inhale all that love and exhale it to the invisibles. In the end, we form a kingdom of breathers of Eternal and Divine love.

And for some of you reading this, perhaps you could be so spiritually exalted and already not be of this world that most people truly do not understand you. They do not have the spiritual orientation to divine your heart and soul, nor the eyes and the attendant heart to recognize reverence and sacredness. Often, they have destroyed these traits in themselves, are racked with guilt and self-hatred and will use you as a scapegoat. They will project onto you all the hatred for themselves they cannot bear to internalize. Pray for them. Pray for their deliverance from the pain that keeps them shackled to their inauthentic selves.

And above all, know that there are some of you on earth who are so exceptional in your spiritual evolution in Christ's domain, that it is only God who can understand you. Know that the greatest phenomenon in existence is the only person capable of understanding you. And what He understands, He loves unconditionally. When you know you have a voice, and no one seems to want to hear it, pray aloud to God and know that your prayers and the sound of your voice are music to His ears.

God loves your voice, and He wants to hear from you.

Prayer for Those Suffering From Work Addiction
and the Tyranny of Their Ambitions:

Dear God:

There are people, especially in the United States, who suffer from work addiction, and from the tyranny of their ambition. As we read this, many of those people have succumbed to life-numbing metaphysical exhaustion. It is an exhaustion that generates a perverse fuel that drives people to a continuous cycle of addition: destructive repetitive behavior—all to fill a void they are helpless at satiating.

I can remember being a work addict. I needed to be a high achiever all my life. The tyranny of my ambitions meant, at times, that I would ignore the internal breakdown of my physical body and treat my body like a machine to achieve goals. During my atheism, once the goals were achieved, I'd feel melancholic and unfulfilled—hungry and insatiable for some greater high. The pursuit of the goals was an intense high; it was intoxicating. My workaholism, Lord, stemmed from the fact that I felt I had to atone for what I believed was the uselessness of my father's life. His lack of achievement, his abysmal failures at every secular pursuit he sought. His schizophrenia, his madness and psychosis—they all haunted me. His glory I would achieve so he could vicariously live through them. More importantly, I felt like a piece of crap who had to justify his existence by achieving. I would be remiss to dismiss my mother's dramatic renditions of her difficult unfair life. And the day, in reference to me and my brother and her mother, she declared as a frustrated divorcee that no man would ever want to marry her because they are aware of the shit she comes with.

It is a memory indelibly imprinted on my consciousness. It is, God, one of the cruelest things a mother could utter to a child. I have never gotten over that evening nor the hateful utterance from my mother's mouth. I would transform myself from a piece of crap into gold through the achievements of my mind. I would hand my mother the glory as an artist, philosopher, and writer my father had only dreamed about. Like a shark, I felt if I were not moving, I would die. I was moving in the direction of success and ambition, and goal realization, and even re-stylizing my life as if I were a consciously willed work of art. The seeds of turning into an accomplishment addict were planted. When you are a young child and your parent (in a state of utter depressive despair) eviscerates you by devaluing herself because you are part of her life, and she believes that her station in life will render her unmarriageable by the majority of men she meets, a part of your innocence is killed. A part of my innocence was killed. Regardless, Lord, of the pressing psychological tensions pulling her into the ground, I believe a mother's first obligation is to protect her young, not attack them in their innocence.

The experience is driven so deep into my consciousness that I feel numb just thinking about it. But there must be inside of me a little boy hurting at being referred to as baggage and "shit." Hurting and screaming in rage and anger. But I don't feel it except in my dreams of anger where the anger is directed at my mother. Forgive her Lord for that act of cruelty. Grant me the grace also to forgive her before she dies. She did not mean to hurt me. Somebody hurt her in a bad manner. Let me magnify her life with the light of my compassion and forgiveness.

I pray for those suffering from the addiction of the tyranny of their ambitions which tells them a lie: that sustained self-love is to be found in the pursuit and achievement of egoic goals. This is a big lie.

Give those suffering from work addiction and the illusion that the short-term satisfaction from filling the void through an orgy of work is worth pursuing the wisdom to know better.

Let them realize that it is only Your abiding love, and their response to Your endless pursuit of them that constitute a lifestyle worthy of living. Fill them with an overabundance of Your being, God, so they come to feel your presence in their souls, not as a perception apart from them, but as the total habitation of Your soul through their searching, yearning, restless spirit.

Give us the strength to move into Your Spirit. We do this, not as a thought or in thought but, rather, as a natural movement of the soul and body in total alignment to where you are located in *this moment* in our lives.

Give us the will and desire to know You as you know Yourself, Lord. To this end, help us to transform ourselves into You by mirroring and then possessing and inhabiting the Spirit of Christ. It is only as You are, God made into man that we can possess You and know You as You are and more: the human face to your infinite obscurity as God in three persons by existing as one nature.

We come to know you through experience and acquaintanceship with your Son. You know us as Jesus knows us in our bare naked egoic humanity. Not as some transcendental oddity. Not by embracing esoteric metaphysical doctrines that Church Fathers themselves cannot fathom but impose, nevertheless, on their human communities as the unassailable moral mandates as pre-requisites for being *seen* by You. You made us. You saw us before we were formed in the womb. We need not do anything for You to see us. We are obliged to transform ourselves and to honor our intrinsic dignity and moral worth and exercise our God-given agency in a manner that would please You—before we present ourselves to You. For in Your majesty and sacredness, we should be at our best when we present ourselves to You.

If in our naked singularity we can present ourselves to You as I did in seeking You, then You will appear. You will enter our souls with Your benevolent light. And in the space that is the void, we will feel much hope.

Those of us addicted to work because of the void must go into the void—jump into the abyss and plummet the darkness. Beneath consciousness lies an undiscovered self that already resides in You; our *not-yet-self*, our self in becoming. Give us the courage and the faith to know that we will find You in the deep depths and there we shall find the unknown and undiscovered selves we have never been acquainted with. We can only find that part of ourselves in You because it is You who are the repository of that authentic self.

Then we will have found a new self, and a new sense of glory that has its source in the great participation of You in our innermost interiority. The self that it is not yet already a self, is realized in You. In the loneliness that drives the addiction, let us glimpse that not-yet-self in its realized form. Let us pray that it is a better self into which we have grown. May this better self be a guide acting under the auspices of You who are able to heal the trauma and injury that created the void that drove the addiction. May that future self through Christ, forgive us of the injurious inflictions of our egoic consciousness against our souls. Let us learn that we do not have to punish ourselves for existing. We exist as a creation of God, and we do not have to justify it. God makes no such demand of us. No rational and benevolent God could do so.

Dear God:

I do think that You love us in all our messiness and basic humanity rather than as some transformed and transcendental oddity. This is why achievement of moral excellence through our virtues practiced in our characters cannot diminish us in our own sight. The imprimatur of Your smile imprinted on our minds; the insignia of a pleased God stamped in our souls should not induce shame and unworthiness when thinking of appearing before You, Lord.

I should stand, with my head held high, shoulders back, palms outward, facing the universe—and feel a sense of exaltation, reverence, esteem, gratitude, humility towards You, our Creator. We should know that you will be pleased by our sacred efforts to exercise our moral agency. Free will you endowed me with. My moral agency and my choice to exercise it, have brought me where I am.

In Your bountiful love, I do not experience You as distant. I feel You as a personal God. If my inner, hidden self, inhabits the spirit of Christ why should I feel debased before You? I do not feel You hiding in the mysterium as some theologians claim you are doing. This feeling in people is the result of a paucity of imagination and a lack of creativity. They don't know that You are rarely, if ever, in the shadows of any aspect of their lives. You are pure light. And You are so bright and transparent that people have reduced You to nothing but a dim perspective. Then theologians write treatises about the hiddenness of You and shadows and inherent invisibility of Your being. What malarkey, written by people who refuse to look at the illuminated torch right before their eyes.

You are not hiding darkness—which is nothing but the absence of light; and You are an abundance of light. You are openly transparent and relentlessly pursuing us and revealing Yourself to us in many ways.

In several ways You are a compound revelation, not just a singular one. You materialize yourself in group scenarios that play themselves out over time. We are co-imbricated in the consequences. We are the legatees and sacred beneficiaries of the judgments and decisions of the conversations of others who stand outside our orbit.

God:

I do believe that reason and the operations of natural law are the highest attributes You possess. And I think that reason is our highest attribute because it points us to Your moral laws independently of faith. Yet those who think that *thought* is the final installment in the pursuit of oneness-with-You transcendence are misguided. Thought will always be incomplete, non-immutable and truncated. Apollonian clarity is not necessarily the goal. To see clearly and not experience even a patina of Your presence is to live with half a soul.

Dear God:

There is this one question I have wanted to ask of You for quite some time. Are You immutable and non-changing? Did Jesus come to redeem the world of its sins—but also to transform you from a jealous, vengeful, and wrathful God of destruction and creation into one of pure love, compassion, and forgiveness? For You made man as a different God. There are no condemnations and inflictions of death and mayhem arising from You. You are superseded by a gentle and inclusive God. Was it Yourself you were trying to soften, to emerge into a new incarnation? For the Son who sits at the right hand of You the Father takes moral precedence over You his Father as a moral figure in Christianity. Often it is to Jesus to whom the Christian sensibilities are often directed. I often miss You, the God of vengeance and justice in the Old Testament. Nowhere are You to be found in the New Testament. Softened and made more temperate by the presence of your Son, You seem metamorphosized into another being who is transported to another world. So, my question is: Did you go through a personality change after your Son was born?

Are You truly immutable and unchanging? Are You hurt by the iniquitous behavior of the world? Or, since You knew each child before it was formed in its mother's womb, and since Your omniscience gives You a clear picture of what man will do with his free will, can You be made distraught by what You know will be the inevitable outcome of the choices and actions of Your creations?

Dear Lord:

In your sermon on the mount, You entreat your followers to not resist evil persons and to, rather, turn the other cheek when struck by an adversary, to carry a soldier's gear for two miles when he requests that we carry it for a mile. If we are sued in court, You say, and our shirt is taken, then we should give our coat.

By what right, Lord? What is the purpose in not resisting evil? And what is the moral reason for not judging while we are here on earth? How do we stop child sex trafficking and child betrothal, and systemic rape as a war crime, and the conscription of children into armies as killers? Must we not judge those who effect such heinous evil in the world as wrong? Must we not defend ourselves from untoward physical incursions against our bodily integrity and those who would eviscerate us of our dignity? Why would You entreat us to be complicit in the harm that others would inflict on us? Help me to understand your moral reasoning here, Lord. If I am struck in the face by a man with full aforethought of malice to belittle and demean me—to harm me, what virtue could possibly lie in inviting him to twice or thrice repeat the insult and harm? What sin is there in protecting myself? Is my life worth less than his? Is my life worth nothing at all? Is it not worth defending? If You gave me precious life and made me in Your image, then why should I sit passively and allow another to harm and damage the image in which I was made by turning the other cheek?

Perhaps it is to shore up the smallness of the attacker and to reveal my dignity and strength by turning the other check. I carry the presence of the Lord within me, so no mortal man can truly eviscerate me of my dignity—only I can perform that feat. Perhaps, I am so possessed of inner peace and strength that in turning the other check I show the bully, the attacker, what a small and insignificant wretch he is when he tries to eviscerate a child of God.

Still, I need to achieve greater clarity of perspective on this issue. I need a deeper sense of discernment regarding its tenability in my life or the life of any person with even a patina of self-respect. If I had a child and I saw someone slapping her, I would never wish for her to turn the other check as a moral response. My love for her would demand that I rush to protect her or equip her to defend herself by neutralizing her attacker. If You love Your children, why would You wish them to invite more abuse into their lives from human abusers?

And further, You say: "Do not judge others, and you will not be judged. For you will be treated as you treat others. The standard you use in judging, is the standard by which you will be judged."

I ask you Lord: What's wrong with judging others in the name of achieving moral, political, and social justice? Were there no judgments cast by men against other men, then blacks would still be enslaved by whites, and slavery would be the order of the day; Hitler would have rapaciously marched over Europe had some men not said: This is an evil man. He must be stopped. We judge Joseph Stalin for his war crimes which included starving thirty million kulak peasants to death. We judge criminals and put them away in prison because they are a threat to society and often to humanity. We judge the men who commit genocide as evil and wrong. We stop them. And yes, those of us who are rational would want to be judged by the same objective and rational and fair standards by which we judge others, for no decent man would wish to commit wrong and walk through the world as a moral cheater and not be held accountable. Why should any honest man who judges by the integrity of his conscience in the name of what he knows to be right and moral wish to escape judgment by others by standards that are objective, fair, and just?

It seems to me Lord, that the preternatural desire not to be judged arises from a disposition that is rotten to the core. It emanates from a person who, as an adult, revels in the unconditional love of others. This desire, God, I believe is nothing more than a lazy desire to remain rooted in one's rottenness. To go on being a garden lout without aspiring to become a better person, all the while hankering after a desire to be loved for one's flaws (not in spite of them) but precisely for them. To say: This is who I am, and I will not change, and you must love me in all my spiritual tawdriness and moral bankruptcy.

I believe, Lord, that only young children who have little control over their moral faculties and agency should ever be loved unconditionally. Those who have control over their agency and who willfully engage in moral slothfulness cannot expect the unearned in matters of love. It mocks the integrity and efforts of those who are morally ambitious and efficacious. If those who are morally evil are loved as deeply as those who are moral aspirants, then what would incentivize the aspirants to become morally ambitious and strive for moral perfection? Why would they waste their time?

Father God:

I pray for those who, like me today, feel overwhelmed with the vicissitudes of life, its challenges and harshness, who feel adrift and a bit lost. And, more importantly, those like me who seem unable to find You in the noise and chaos of modern life. I pray that they see Your face and feel Your presence in the gesture of another. For those who feel they cannot find You, I pray that they re-conceive their purpose in life to one in which purpose is articulated as identifying the gift we have inside ourselves and applying them to the needs of those in our communities, or anyone in the world who has a need to be met. Then everyone will have a purpose as there will always be a need to be met, and we will always find within ourselves a talent, a gift, a part of ourselves to offer that can heal and fill the void in another.

It is there, I hope and pray that we will find Your presence both in the giving and in the gratitude offered by those to whom we give. And should gratitude not be forthcoming, that will be alright. We see and feel Your presence in the vitality and exuberance that reverberate through our bodies as our hearts—broken but still beating—extend themselves in communion and love to those of others.

Prayer for Those Suffering in Times of War, Hunger, and Homelessness:

Dear God:

Today I ask You to extend the hand of healing and serenity to those suffering around the world from the ravages of war, hunger, and homelessness. I have no idea how this prayer will progress, for in my finiteness I would not know what to say to such people ensconced in such despair and abject hopelessness.

Lord, sit with them in their despair as You would with a friend in need. Let them feel your presence, and in You, let them sense an anchor—an unchanging and immutable consistency. As the vagaries of their lives change from hour to hour and day by day, ensconce Yourself in their hearts and give them the feeling: *I am not alone.* Comfort them the way we are all comforted by being in nature: by the sweet sounds of birds singing, and waters running incandescently over rocks in a surging stream; or the sense of equanimity we feel when we gaze out at the vastness of a calm ocean or a still lake. Be that rock for them. Let them know that they are rooted in a time and place that is your eternal kingdom. It is unchanging. It is an oasis. Give them some access to that world and let them be nourished by the peace that is a founding feature of Your world.

Let Your presence and love and serenity supersede their despair and hopelessness. Let the inevitable sense of hope that resides in each one of us rise in them. Give them the gift of surrendering to what is their fate in the present moment, and the courage to believe in the endless possibilities of a future that You can lay open for them.

Dear God:

Give us all the insight to understand why low-quality socializing is never as good as high-quality solitude. Help us to understand that such solitude is not self-referential, and is not ego directed; rather, it is a solitude that meditates on the self-possessive and self-contained nature of the self that grounds itself in the light of Your love and presence. It is a solitude that reflects on and ponders the nature of our presence inside the matrix of Your infiniteness. In our solitude, we find ourselves being stretched to the outer and inner infinite possibilities and ranges of becoming the Godly human in which You made us. Solitude is that milieu in which spaces open up for us, where silence breathes heretofore unseen visions of who we might yet become as unrevealed images You hold of us that are yet to be revealed manifest themselves. We ideate and become through Your revelations away from the noises and distractions of the modern world.

Help us to understand that low-quality socializing necessitates the absence of growth for it is repetition of the old and dated self that cannot and will not respond to new challenges and obstacles and, therefore, usher in the face of our limitless humanity. Hubris and laziness force us to codify and then canonize our canned responses to life's challenges and proffer rote responses to human dilemmas: those of our families, friends, loved ones and, more importantly—our own. Solitude can be that space of loving self-confrontation where the void and abyss open and we feel the concatenations of linked events that tie our lives into a compartmentalized theme. Solitude can give us pause. It can lovingly move us to morally thematize our lives by a single moral thread that leads back to you. When we examine our lives, we don't see a discombobulated disunited and unconnected piecemeal situational ethical framework that threads our lives as if they are lived episodically. Rather, we are steered in a direction that forces us to see our lives like wholesalers rather than retailers in the realm of morality, as comprehensive and universal in our reach to you. We witness the integration of our lives by your unifying laws and mandates.

In low-quality socializing we are looking for some semblance of happiness outside of You. That happiness is ephemeral, provisional, and contingent. Solitude gives us the space to discern and then experience the fact that outside of participation in Your Holy Presence and Divine Being—there can be no understanding. We reach a spiritual cul-de-sac, and the only exit is on the wings of Your love that flies us to a completely different world.

Father God:

I had a conversation with my mother regarding those who decide to end their lives with the help of what some call *assisted suicide*. They do this because, indeed, you have given them more than they can bear! They are physically terminally ill, consumed by indescribable and unbearable pain; or their minds are ravaged by terminal diseases and unspeakable suffering. They writhe in agony, lie in their filth, and feel eviscerated of their dignity. They simply cannot see where there is to get to. Hope is lost. The future? They cannot see it. They want to die with dignity.

What could be wrong with pursuing such a choice? There is a popular canard: *God never gives us more than we can bear.* I do not believe the seven-year-old girl sold into sex slavery and gang-raped and tortured several times a day for several months has any use for that slogan. That is more than she can bear. Later she grows up damaged. The humiliation, the scars and the wounds are too much. The abyss and the void consume her. Her dignity and innocence have been sullied. She has been afflicted with more than she can tolerate. The world closes in on her and suffocates her. She takes her life at thirty, unable to withstand the suffering any longer. By what right can anyone blame, judge, and condemn her? On what grounds could You convict her when You did not intervene in her rape and torture?

I trust, God, that others will not say that in the manner of death inflicted upon Your Son—death by crucifixion—that he, too, was eviscerated of his dignity. It was a death he participated in to fulfill the scriptures. He was God made man. He was a God. He performed miracles and raised the living from the dead. He was no ordinary man. Mortal man cannot be expected, I believe, God, to endure the challenges and sufferings endured by a Man-God. The asymmetry between Christ and mortal man is so gargantuan that we can only approximate Christ's moral perfection and psychological grandeur.

But returning to the issue of assisted suicide or moral suicide for the purpose of dying with dignity, I would say You gave us free will. A rational appraisal of our condition could lead some to believe that they are constitutionally unable to bear their suffering any longer; or, that the abject state of continued degradation that characterizes their lives renders them paralyzed, and hopeless beyond reach. They cannot find You although they have tried. My thoughts are that You gave us free will to place in the service of our lives. Had You not wanted us to use that free will—even in a manner that contradicted Your will—then You would not have given us that free will to use at our discretion and according to our own discernment—flawed as it might be. If free will is a gift from You, as I believe it is, then we have a moral responsibility to use it and bear the consequences of exercising it in a way that is not consistent with Your wishes, even as we pray fervently that our will be may be reconciled with Yours, and that our actions be aligned with Your vision for what is ultimately best for us.

Prayer for Those Who Have Committed Psychological Suicide:

Dear God:

There are those among us who walk in a state of soullessness. They have not sold their souls to anyone. They were not born without souls. They are mired in deep contempt for a world they see as irresolutely bankrupt and evil, and destructive of all goodness. They kill their capacity to cope with the world. They do not think that virtue can survive the onslaughts of depravity and moral rot that have enveloped the world. They give greater psychological credence to the idea that evil will consume goodness; vulgarity will crush refinement; and malevolence will make civility and benevolence irrelevant among humans. They turn against their own idealism that is marinated in the highest possible which exists—which is You.

Some have been mangled by failed relationships, with lovers, ex-spouses, children, and family. No price is worthy of their conscience; and to kill themselves would be to miss out on the slightest of chances that some renaissance of the spirit might occur. They have killed themselves psychologically so they may be the first to inflict on themselves the worst that the world has to offer. Some become antisocial, others addicted to alcohol, prescription and recreational drugs. Some are just exhausted, Lord. Tired of simply existing: The weight of life crushes up against them.

This sickness which is truly despair has no end once the world unravels and they are here—with much reverence in their souls—to perceive the putrefaction that gasses their lives as they try to breathe and just be still.

To the living dead among us God, I ask that You restore their physical and emotional vitality and their exuberance by first awakening their capacity to see the beauty all around them: the God in You that exists in all persons. Let them see— those who are murdering their own souls–Your resplendent light radiating even in the worst and least among us. Our souls are just looking for a community.

Let the soul killers awaken from their spiritual and secular slumber and see that in You, we have a God-soul derived from being made in Your image. And with that God-soul You have granted us the permission to unleash our godliness in all spheres of life. God, I pray that those who have mangled their souls, a mangling forged in the crucibles of shame, guilt, disappointments and, of being truly victimized by others in the world, will find strength in Your will and Your personal revelation of You in their lives. Let them see that it is not the world that is stacked against them. Rather, it is they who have been addicted to the ephemeral, the temporary, and the episodic. If they lack faith, then give them the burning sensation and instinct that something higher exists, something more exalted and passionate. God, I ask that You imbue them with—in this hour of reading—the conviction that You are the ideal. You are the consummate hero they should be reflecting on. In You they will find no betrayal; no abandonment, and no backstabbing. Because standing in the way of all assaults and attacks stands an everlasting image and figure who has already fought the battles for them, suffered the assaults, insults, and abuse on their behalf. And now, we pray to Him to remind them of these key words: "No weapon formed against me shall prosper". And we pray these words and ask for comfort and solace for those among us afflicted with suicide of the soul.

Dear God:

Once more, I want to visit the Garden of Eden and talk about what happened there. We know You forbade Adam and Eve to eat of the Tree of Knowledge.

I return to the issue of You having made man—Adam and Eve—in Your own image. It means that You who are omniscient and omnipotent, would genetically pass on to your children the striving for power and knowledge. They will display Your attributes! The attributes of God the Creator. What Adam and Eve gained in their Edenic bliss was that which You sought to deny them: knowledge and ethical sensitivity as this would have led to their creativity and would have put them in the position of thinking that they could compete with You. All creative endeavors are accompanied by a maniacal impulse to outdistance others. Don't you agree, Lord?

What was you motive in making us in Your image with all the concomitant aspirational features that would accompany a human-God-made person? Why did You seek to keep us in a state of psychic infantilism, of never knowing the full scale of our human capabilities? Why did You desire to keep us in a state of infantile bliss? Why did You create children whom You never intended to mature and grow up and question that which they perceived? Why give us free will if in using it—a constitutive attribute You endowed us with—we usher in the fall of man? If You are all powerful and all-knowing, what Edenic delights could You have derived from contemplating the spectacle of mindless automatons in total devotion to your wishes, to keep us locked in childhood? What parent does not wish for his or her child to become aware of him or herself, to grow out of psychological infancy, and to exercise his or her physical and mental capabilities? What parent wants to bind his or her children in such intimate proximity and have them remain children for life?

If we are made in Your image and eat of the Tree of Knowledge, then any aspirational quest realized in life would be a mere plagiarism against you—an approximation of the perfect form that You are.

Is it that what You were saving man from?

But the decision of Adam and Eve to eat of the Tree of Knowledge spoke to their awareness of themselves as individuated self-reflecting beings. There must have been a longing to discover, to know something more; and, You must have planted that desire in them: the desire to go beyond infant curiosity to deeper striving for consciousness and the emancipation from eternal incurred tutelage on You. This striving to become, to imitate the pure being You are, to aspire to God-head—are all modes of being they carried in them and that drove them to eat in and of life. And if You made them with such capabilities then You must have known the stirrings that would accompany Your planted modes of being and becoming in your creation.

Adam and Eve became human beings rather than remain innocent infants. You punished them with the cravings for sexual desire and the need to work. But, God, it is through productive work that we learn the virtues that lead to us support our own lives. Who but a worthless neurotic would see work—the need to use one's own efforts (reason and labor) to sustain one's life—as a curse?

My final question to You is this: Did you intend to have Adam and Eve remain child-like automatons or, without their act of disobedience, did You have another plan for them to grow into free and illustrious beings? Why was the fall of man such a severe one that sprang from, as far as I can see, a simple desire to grow up?

Dear God: (An Apology)

May I say I am sorry. I apologize. I apologize for all the goodness that You bestowed on my life for which I took credit. In my unmitigated hubris there were times when You steered the course of my life in ways I could not have imagined. There were existential dilemmas that plagued my life, roadblocks that threatened my future. I found myself surrounded by insurmountable problems that threatened to unravel my carefully crafted goals and my well-thought-out aspirations. Blocks appeared and I had no idea how I would ever find a solution to removing them. I did not believe in Your existence. When the solutions mysteriously appeared not once but on innumerable occasions, I chalked them up to the power of my will to alter the nature of the universe! My will! My will!

How do I see now, how You always had my back even as I chastised those who praised and glorified Your name. These letters explain a lot of my foolish ways. But an apology is in order. And gratitude, Lord—deep gratitude I offer now to You humbly for taking such good care of my life; for shepherding my dreams, restoring me to health when my surgery went awry, and I almost died. And regrettably, on that night when I categorically did not want to live, and I swallowed some pills with a bottle of wine. You blew life into me and gave me strength to plant my feet firmly on the ground the following morning. Like the fox, I looked for the ground and kept on running. I am no longer running, Lord. Just walking patiently towards You. Even when I feel I have lost You, my faith grows stronger, and I walk in silence and in gratitude. My love for You grows with each passing day. You are exciting. Life can never be boring because you are the infusion in all life.

Bless and unite our amazing country, Lord: The United States of America. Let all Americans look upon each other and recognize the God that resides in each of them. Help us to put aside our political differences, and will and affirm in Godly benevolence, the flourishing and well-being of our fellow compatriots. Help us to learn to love and affirm the intrinsic moral dignity of each other.

Regardless of who our president is, bless and guide that person to lead us into continued prosperity, peace, and unity.

Thank you, God, for my life. And thank you with all my heart for my existence upon this earth of yours.

Dearest God:

Our journey through these epistolary outpouring of questions, deliberations, speculations, prayers, devotionals and, Your answers, have all come to an end. You taught me how to pray through my hands and fingers. For now, I must pause and rest in contemplation of You, in gratitude that You chose me and granted me grace. I rejected You, and You sat with me and embraced me in Your loving presence.

This is not goodbye, Lord. It is the prolegomenon to our newly consecrated union.

How I long to be a supplicant for You, to wake and serve Your will, to have Your paean hymns engraved in my throat. They are there, Lord.

And now: To hear melodious incantations, sighs, chants, and harmonious yearnings make me sob.

I walk and face the world as I did when I was a child; when I knew who I was before the world tried to intervene and tell me who I had to become. I walk with renewed innocence and hopefulness. I embrace Your gentle touch, and I feel the tingling in my heart when I think of You, when I speak of you. I am excited when I think of the life I most want: to be a writer exalting your name and glory.

I walk and dance and prance and think: *I am afraid to confess any of this to the world; but, I know that among the deepest of ways to communicate my love for You is writing to You.* It is in writing that I locate the tipping point in my soul, and only from that precarious point where I do my balancing act and sing out my refrain of joy that have I any right to seek You.

Lord, You alone make me happy. And so, I know this for sure, and I will proclaim it to all who will hear me:

Lamentation is the voice of God writing His hymns into our hearts.

Jubilation is the cry of God as He rejoices in our personal victories.

Sadness is His sigh at the pain He feels in witnessing our privations.

Silence is His permanent presence in our souls.

All My Love,

Your son,

Jason